HAROLD REDUX

HAROLD REDUX

THOMAS FASANO

COYOTE CANYON PRESS
CLAREMONT, CA

Copyright © 2025 by Thomas Fasano

All rights reserved.

No part of this publication may be reproduced, distributed, or transmitted in any form or by any means, including photocopying, recording, or other electronic or mechanical methods, without the prior written permission of the author, except in the case of brief quotations embodied in critical reviews and certain other noncommercial uses permitted by copyright law.

Paperback ISBN: 979-8-9877655-5-5

First Edition

Canto the First
I.

O Muse, embalmed in Botox, ash, and gin,
Who ghosted Delphi's Yelp page long ago,
Your shrine is shuttered—only spam gets in—
No Instagram can resurrect its glow.
I scroll the ruins; the algorithm knows,
Suggesting saints, whores, supplements, and grief.
But I—your bingeing pilgrim—hunger grows:
To post my sorrow like a stolen motif,
And hashtag my decline with filtered disbelief.

II.

Once, in the island once called Albion,
A youth streamed chaos, nihilist and raw;
His Netflix queue was riot, Babylon,
His laughter pissed against each fragile law.
No virtue swiped right—vice alone he saw;
In strip clubs, bathhouses, the rave's dim tomb,
He feasted, sleepless, gulping molly's draw—
Till dawn revealed the selfies of his doom,
His face a glitching mask, mid-orgy, mid-Zoom.

III.

He called himself Childe Harold—who can say
If Harold was his Uber-handle, fake?
His fathers, once Olympian, fell away,
Like crypto coins in some spectacular break.
The brand was tarnished, nothing left to stake;
No ghostwriter, no hagiography,
Could scrub the stains his gaping scandals make.
Fame curdles, rancid as pornography;
Sin's livestream leaves no room for elegy.

IV.

He basked beneath a cruel, indifferent sun,
A fly that twitched upon the mirrored glass;
The world was ending, but the memes were fun,
The death-feed scrolling, endless as the mass
Of headlines promising the storm to pass.
Yet every noon became a neon night,
Where hunger turned to vomit, gold to brass;
Satiety, that corpse in candlelight,
Betrayed him to himself—a relic, post-fortnite.

V.

Through sin's unholy labyrinth he ran,
A rave-lit maze of strangers, lovers, loss;
He kissed one ghost but groped another's hand,
His love a credit card declined, a cross.
The girl he worshipped, lucky to be lost,
Escaped the rot that would have made her prey.
Her beauty, fragile as a shard of gloss,
He would have pawned for bottle service pay,
And left her in the ruins of his wasted day.

VI.

Now Harold sickened of the endless rave,
The Bacchic crew whose joy was rented breath;
A prideful tear was something he forgave
Himself in secret, wept in stealth of death.
Alone he wandered, starving for the meth
Of sorrow's sting, or even woe's cheap high.
He longed to flee his homeland's stagnant heft—
To sweat in jungles, burn beneath the sky,
Or crawl to Hades' gate for just a change of eye

VII.

He ghosted from his father's crumbling hall,
A relic, gothic, half condemned, half chic;
The pillars leaned, as if they knew the fall
Was imminent, yet stubborn, antique, bleak.
What once was prayer was now a strip-club streak:
Where monks had fasted, Paphian girls sang loud,
Their bodies lit like idols for the weak.
The past returned, absurdly, in that crowd,
Where sacred vows were mocked, defiled, and disavowed.

VIII.

Yet sometimes in the hangover of cheer,
A pang of something nameless seized his brow;
As if a feud, long buried, whispered near,
Or some rejected lover cursed him now.
But Harold's soul was not the kind to vow
Its grief to friends, nor spill a single tear;
He locked the hurt away, a hidden Tao,
A viral wound, a secret engineered,
A silence swallowed whole, a sickness never cleared.

IX.

And none did love him! Though his parties burned
With sycophants in borrowed, rented glow,
He knew their praise was counterfeit, well-learned—
A parasitic cheer, a plastic show.
The women came for power, fame, and flow,
Not Harold's broken, vacant, midnight eyes.
Where Mammon beckons, moths of beauty go;
Even angels falter, compromise,
And love becomes a ghost, a bribe, a thin disguise.

X.

He had a mother once—though best forgot,
For tenderness was something he had fled.
A sister too, beloved—but he sought
No last embrace before his exile spread.
His friends, if such existed, thought him dead,
And Harold left without a single wave.
Yet partings weigh like stone upon the head
Of those who dream a bond survives the grave;
Love's wound, once cauterized, still weeps for what it gave.

XI.

His house, a mausoleum dressed in glass,
Where heiresses once cooed in champagne light,
And saints were shaken by each pert, false lass
Whose lips were glossed for Instagram's delight;
The goblets brimmed with every costly blight.
The fleet of vintages, the Persian rugs,
The Hermes leash for every passing night—
He left it all, like Gucci-bagged young thugs,
To chase the world's disease, its hashtags and its drugs.

XII.

The sails were filled; the paparazzi's breeze
Seemed glad to waft him from his native shame;
The cliffs dissolved in foamy photorelease,
White rocks became a background, not a name.
Regret might stir, but Harold played the game;
No whimper, though his entourage was weeping.
His lips stayed mute, his heart a brand aflame;
While others mourned the home they'd not be keeping,
He scrolled in silence, doomscrolled past the grief of sleeping.

XIII.

At sunset, when the ocean flamed with rust,
He seized a harp—his feed, his silver string.
He plucked at notes as any vagrant must,
Untutored, shy, yet desperate to sing.
His farewell tuned itself in twilight's ring;
The vessel surged, its snowy wing a lie.
And fading shores, like mothers vanishing,
Were swallowed whole; he gave his last goodbye,
A ballad poured to waves, to drones, to sea, to sky.

1.

"Adieu, adieu! my native shore departs,
Drowned in the filters blue;
The gulls cry hashtags, breakers tear apart,
The meme becomes the true.
That sun, descending, ghosts his own domain,
And I, his feckless knight,
Say farewell once again to earth and pain,
My homeland—good good night."

2.

"A few short hours, he'll rise in pixel flame,
And crown tomorrow's birth;
Yet I shall wake to ocean's blank arcade,
And not my mother earth.
The halls are vacant, shutters fall to weeds,
The hearth is cold with hate;
A dog, half-starved, still howls for vanished deeds,
Alone beside the gate."

3.

'Come here, my page,' he said, 'why weep and quake?
The gale is only air.
Our ship is swift, a falcon in its wake—
The storm is hardly there.'
But still the child wept, still he would not smile,
And Harold mocked his tone:
"You've lost a mother, father—stay a while,
You've still got me... and One."

4.

The page replied: "My father blessed me sore,
But mother will not rest;
She sighs till I return, and evermore
She clutches at her breast.
Enough, enough! I cannot bear your cheer,
Sir Harold, if I try;
If I possessed your cynic's heart of sneer,
Mine own would not run dry."

5.

"Come hither, yeoman, staunch and pale with dread,
What makes thy color fade?
The French, the gale, the future, or the dead?"
'No, sir, I'm not afraid.
But wife and boys remain beside your hall,
Their cries will pierce my head;
When they shall call, and I can answer not,
She'll curse me as if dead.'

6.

"Enough, enough, my loyal yeoman good—
But know, I flee with laughs.
Your wife will find a fresher paramour,
Her tears are epitaphs.
For pleasures past I do not mourn nor wail,
Nor fear the perils near;
My grief is simply that my tale
Leaves nothing left to tear."

7.

And so he laughed, the exile, all alone,
Adrift upon the sea;
For why should he take others' grief as stone,
When none would sigh for he?
Perchance the starving dog at gate would pine,
Till strangers threw their hands;
But long before his bark should whine,
He'd rip his master's brands.

8.

Then Harold turned to waves and sang anew:
"My bark, my floating stage—
I care not where you bear me, false or true,
Past countries, past an age.
Welcome, dark caverns, deserts, tombs of light,
Where I may lose my name;
Farewell, my homeland, swallowed into night,
My birthplace, ghost, and shame."

XIV.

The vessel lurched; the land was gone for good,
In Biscay's sleepless rave the gales were mean.
By day four Harold starved for holy food,
But on the fifth the coastline split the screen:
Cintra's mountains, Tagus, gold obscene,
Where fables promised wealth and kingship's trust.
The pilots leapt aboard with practiced sheen,
And steered through shores where peasants, choking dust,
Reaped little from the soil, though born to God and rust.

XV.

O Christ! how lush the filtered land appears,
A panorama fit for Apple screens;
The groves of fragrance glisten through the tears
Of tourists drunk on hashtagged travel scenes.
But man, forever armed with crude machines,
Would desecrate what Heaven once had made;
And when the lash descends for such routines,
The Gaul shall swarm, a locust cavalcade,
And purge the spoiled earth with debt no saint has paid.

XVI.

Lisboa lifts her face upon the tide,
A queen whose portrait swims in pixel gold.
A thousand keels parade her bloated pride,
Alliance bought, allegiance quickly sold.
The Lusians—ignorant, vain, and bold—
Still lick the hand that shields them from the foe;
They loathe the sword, but cannot break its hold,
Despising all the might that saves them so—
A nation proud in shame, a pageant staged for show.

XVII.

But enter in the town, celestial bright,
And wander lost among its filth and cries;
For hut and palace share the same sad blight,
And dirt is sovereign—virtue never buys.
The people, clothed in stains and sour disguise,
Seem raised in gutters, reared on plague and flies.
No class, no crown, no slave nor lord denies
The grime that coats their shirt and trouser thighs;
Yet life goes on unwashed, unshamed, beneath their skies.

XVIII.

Why waste thy marvels, Nature, on these drones?
For Cintra's Eden waits with endless maze—
Of mount and glen where paradise intones
Its riot of disorder and amaze.
What bard, what painter, dares record its gaze,
This dream of light that mocks the mortal pen?
Not even Milton's voice nor Homer's phrase
Could open half the gates to mortal men,
Whose eyes go blind with awe, then stagger shut again.

XIX.

The convent crowns the crags with ruin's weight,
The cork-trees hang, the moss is burned to bone.
The valleys weep, the skies intoxicate,
The azure sea lies stretched, a polished stone.
The orange glows, the torrents moan and groan,
The vines cling high, the willow droops below.
All mingled in a scene that swells alone,
A collage where the colors bleed and glow,
A fevered fresco hung in God's unyielding show.

XX.

Climb slow the winding road, the monks await,
"Our Lady's House of Woe" their bitter sign.
They show their relics, petty, desolate,
Their legends trembling, bloodied yet benign.
Here sinners punished, here did saints repine,
Honorius gnawed himself in cave of stone,
Believing torment would make grace divine.
To merit Heaven he made Hell his own,
And carved a tomb of prayer from marrow, blood, and bone.

XXI.

And crosses crude are carved beside the way,
Not signs of worship but of slaughter done;
For where the victim shrieked, there must one lay
A lath-built token, ghost of murder's fun.
The groves and glens are littered, every one,
With rotten wood that testifies to death.
The land is purple, soaked beneath the sun,
Where law sleeps drunk, where justice holds her breath,
And knives still write their scripture in the blood of Seth.

XXII.

Here kings repaired, but now their halls decay,
The wildflowers bloom where scepters used to reign.
Yet Splendor lingers, ghost of yesterday,
And ruins preach the sermon of the vain.
The palace towers, desolate and slain,
Vathek, thy paradise dissolved in weeds.
When wanton wealth has played its mightiest game,
Peace turns away from such luxurious deeds,
And Time, that butcher, comes to sell his rotten feeds.

XXIII.

Here thou didst dwell, O architect of dream,
And plotted pleasures, schemes of idle hour.
But now thy palace rots, a meme, a meme!
Its fairy dwellings drowned in choking flower.
The portals gape, the halls confess their power
To ruin's touch, and Harold, seeing this,
Bowed to the wreck, a monk within a tower,
And learned the fleeting worth of earthly bliss—
All vanish in the tide, the kiss becomes abyss.

XXIV.

Behold the hall where chieftains lately sat,
A dome displeasing to the British brow.
There squats a demon—Fiend in fool's-format—
With parchment robes and mocking, endless vow.
The seal, the scroll, the names still burn somehow,
But laughter rises, cruel, profane, obscene.
The Urchin points and laughs as if to cow
The lords of fame, the laureled, once serene,
Now signed away in ink to haunt a page unclean.

XXV.

Convention is the name the demon bore,
That foiled the knights in Marialva's dome.
He mocked their laurels, filched their sacred store,
And turned their victory's wine to froth and foam.
Here Folly broke the plume of Albion's home,
And Policy reclaimed what arms had lost.
The laurel's bloom is wasted, poets moan—
For heroes win at unimagined cost,
When Triumph on the shore of Cintra turns to frost.

XXVI.

Since that dark conclave met, Britannia sighs,
And sickens at the whisper of thy name.
The offices, ashamed, avert their eyes,
And curse their shame, though shameless all the same.
How will the future write this tale of shame?
The conquered mocked the conquerors in their turn;
A parchment trumps a battle, what a game!
And Scorn shall point her finger as they burn,
For history writes in bile what men would fain adjourn.

XXVII.

So Harold mused as mountains held his way,
Alone, though bathed in splendor's fevered light.
He thought to flee, more restless day by day,
As swallows dart before the fall of night.
Yet here he paused to moralize, contrite,
And reason whispered through the fog of years,
Despising youth misspent in vain delight.
But truth was fire that scorched his sight with tears,
And dimmed the very eyes that once had scanned his fears.

XXVIII.

To horse, to horse! he fled the scene of balm,
Though sweet its peace, it sickened him at last.
He roused himself from melancholy calm,
No more to seek the harlot or the glass.
But still he roved, with neither home nor past,
No pilgrim's rest, no goal of holy flight.
The world would roll through ever-shifting cast,
Till travel dulled his thirst for transient sight,
Or pain became his guide, or wisdom proved his blight.

XXIX.

Yet Mafra's dome detained his eyes awhile,
Where queens had wailed, where priests and lords conspired.
The Mass and revel mingled in defile,
The sacred vow with lust's profane desired.
Here Babylonian Whore, in gems attired,
Had built her throne, her pomp a bloody cheat.
Men bowed before the glories she acquired,
Forgetting how her hands were stained in meat,
And worshipped at her shrine of varnished, guilty heat.

XXX.

Through valleys fat with fruit and scripted views,
Romantic hills like wallpapers for phones,
Where even sluggards feel a pang, a bruise,
That beauty mocks their ergonomic thrones.
The Childe kept wandering—wandering alone—
Though others sneered that roaming was a crime.
Yet in the mountain air, a truth was sown:
That life, which bloated ease cannot mime,
Is sweeter when inhaled beyond the walls of time.

XXXI.

The hills fell back; the plains spread, bleak and bare,
A Netflix matte of horizon, edge to edge.
The shepherds guarded flocks with brutal care,
For Spain was girded round in iron pledge.
Each lamb was proof against the tyrant's hedge,
Each fleece a coin the trader meant to keep.
The pastor's crook became a soldier's wedge,
For wolves were human, and the vigil deep;
They fought for all they had, or bent the knee to weep.

XXXII.

Where Lusian borders kiss their Spanish kin,
What wall divides, what iron fence is laid?
No Yangtze's flood, no Alps that rise and grin,
No dragon's spine, no barricade displayed.
The queens of earth, so jealous, still are stayed
By less than mountain, river, fort, or wall.
The line is drawn by hate itself, in shade,
Invisible yet stronger than them all,
A border stitched by ghosts, by feud, by Cain's first call.

XXXIII.

Between them slips a nameless trickling stream,
A silver vein no map would deign to show.
Here shepherds lean and drowse, and half in dream
Stare at the ripples' idle, aimless flow.
The brook divides, but cannot truly know
The venom steeped in either peasant's pride.
Each hind believes himself a duke; and lo,
The Spaniard marks the Lusian slave beside,
And thanks his God he's not that low, debased, denied.

XXXIV.

Then Guadiana, swollen, dark, immense,
Rolls on in sullen, restless billowing;
Its waters echo battles, violence—
The Moors, the knights, their bright mail glittering.
Here champions fell, here speed was smothering,
The Paynim turban met the Christian crest.
The river bore their corpses, suffering,
A floating pageant, bloody and unblessed,
A liquid grave where East and West together rest.

XXXV.

O Spain, O lovely, blood-soaked, ruined stage,
Where banners once flamed scarlet in the gale!
Pelagio's hand struck sparks against the age,
And Cava's father's treachery set the tale.
Where now those standards? Where the heroes hale?
The Crescent paled, the Cross at last prevailed.
The wails of Moorish matrons filled the vale,
While Afric's echo endlessly bewailed,
A dirge for vanished power, for victories curtailed.

XXXVI.

What's left? A ditty, echo of the fight.
So much for heroes—this the final fate:
When marble crumbles, when the scrolls turn white,
The peasant's song preserves the doubtful date.
Pride, bow your head! for all is small and late.
The mighty shrink to measures sung in ale.
The books, the tombs, the pillars ornate—
All rot, all sleep. Tradition will prevail,
The last frail tongue repeating what the first let fail.

XXXVII.

Awake, ye Sons of Spain!—your goddess calls,
Though not with lance, nor plumes of scarlet flare.
She rides instead on gunpowder that falls,
On cannon's smoke that blackens out the air.
Her voice is thunder—engineered despair,
Each roar a hymn, each peal a godless prayer.
"Arise, awake!" she shrieks across the square,
Her war-song bending Andalusia bare,
Not trumpets now, but shells, explosions everywhere.

XXXVIII.

Hark! Did you hear the hoofs of dreadful speed,
The sabres whistling through the choking mist?
The brothers fell, unrescued in their need,
The tyrant's lash, the tyrant's slaves assist.
The bonfires rage, the air itself is kissed
By sulfur, blood, by shrieks from cliff to plain.
The volleys thunder, thousands cease, dismissed;
Death gallops swift, his breath a burning chain,
He stamps his foot and all the nations break in pain.

XXXIX.

Look there—the Giant crowns the mountain's face,
His hair aflame, his hands with lightning armed.
His gaze incinerates the fragile race,
His stare itself a judgment, fierce, unharmed.
Destruction crouches at his feet, alarmed,
To watch what he commands in death's domain.
For three great nations meet, their bodies charmed
To pour their blood before this god obscene,
Whose shrine is slaughter, whose delight is human pain.

XL.

By Heaven! what a show, what spectacle,
For one without a brother in the field!
The rival scarves, the arms fantastical,
A carnival of death that will not yield.
The war-hounds gnash their teeth, their joy concealed;
They hunger, howl, they leap to maim, to slay.
But in the grave the choicest prize is sealed,
And Havoc, counting corpses in array,
Can scarcely tally joy for ruin's grand ballet.

XLI.

Three armies kneel to consecrate the dead,
Three tongues intone their glitching, rival prayer;
Three banners bleed their logos overhead—
France, Spain, and Albion, branding their despair.
The foe, the friend, the victim, all are there,
Each livestreaming sacrifice in vain;
They die abroad who might have rotted where
Their cribs were built; instead, on foreign plain,
They fertilize the earth with hashtags of their pain.

XLII.

There rot they now—ambition's honored fools,
Whose turf is stitched with ribbons, false renown.
See honor crown the carcass, honor schools
The clay that Tyrants throw like dice around.
By myriads, broken, human hearts are ground
Beneath the heel of power's dream alone.
And Despots—what? they never hold the ground,
Except the patch of soil that claims their bone,
The plot where all their lies dissolve, each lie dethroned.

XLIII.

O Albuera! field of grief and ghost,
The pilgrim passing could not see thy fate;
How soon thy plain would host a mingled host,
And corpses, trophies, victory's cheap estate.
Peace to the perished! may the singer prate
Their names a while, their meed of song prolong—
Until new legions march to the same gate,
And fresh blood stains the earth with the same wrong,
Their glory shrunk to ink, embalmed in transient song.

XLIV.

Enough of battle's addicts! let them trade
Their lives for trending fame, for tombstone likes.
What does it profit? clay cannot be swayed,
Though tens of thousands fall for one that spikes.
O hirelings, striking blows for nation's pikes,
Whose deaths are claimed as virtue, service, good—
Had you survived, you'd only feed the strikes
Of narrow feud, of rapine's brotherhood;
But dying, you are saints, embalmed in foreign blood.

XLV.

Swift Harold wends where Sevilla still stands,
Unconquered yet, though conquest smells her near.
Is she not free? The Spoiler's blackened hands
Already smudge her domes, her pride austere.
Inevitable hour! To strive is mere
Folly, unless Troy or Tyre might still outlast.
Where famine's brood is planted, fate is clear:
The virtuous fall, the murderers hold fast,
And beauty burns away, as if it never passed.

XLVI.

But knowing not, the city laughs and feasts,
Love's rebeck drowns war's clarion for the night.
The patriots bleed not with their land; the priests
Still bless the wine, the courtesans' delight.
Vice clings, a lover to a corpse's sight,
The capitals enthralled by silent crime.
The orgies drone, the candles flare too bright;
And on the eve of ruin's fatal climb,
The revel masks decay, until the last bell's chime.

XLVII.

Not so the rustic—he with trembling bride
Lurks silent, scanning vineyards, clutching fear.
His vines will shrivel in war's ashen tide,
The hot breath scorches all that once was dear.
No more at dusk the castanet rings clear,
The fandango twirls beneath consenting star.
Ah, kings! if you could taste the mirth you smear,
You'd fling away the iron, burn the scar;
The drum would sleep, and man would laugh beneath his bar.

XLVIII.

How sings the muleteer? Not love, nor prayer,
Nor romance, ringing bells along the road.
No, now he shrieks "¡Viva el Rey!" in glare,
And curses Godoy, bastard king's abode.
The queen's dark boy, her treason's lust corrode,
Spawned gore-faced ruin, born of joy impure.
The song that once could sanctify the load
Now spits at kings, at lust they can't obscure;
Spain's ballads rot with rage, no longer soft, demure.

XLIX.

Across the plain, the hoof-marks scar the soil,
Where Moorish towers crown the crags with flame.
The greensward's charred, a witness to the toil,
The camp, the host, the fire, the fleeting fame.
Here peasants stormed the dragon's den, became
The myth of self, insurgent, bold, and proud.
They mark the cliffs with boast of fight, of claim,
Point out the rocks where victors bled aloud,
And wear the scars of war as peasants' shroud.

L.

Whoe'er you meet will wear the crimson sign,
The badge that brands the loyal from the foe.
Without it, death is quick, the blade will shine,
The poniard hidden strikes its sudden blow.
The Gallic rue the ambush, subtle, low,
That stabs beneath the cloak, behind the smoke.
For cannon thunders, sabres rise and glow,
But sharper still the knife that whispers, broke—
And blood rewrites the law in cities war bespoke.

LI.

At every turn Morena's heights display
The hardware of an empire on the brink—
Howitzers squatting, palisades decay,
The shattered road, the fosse with stagnant stink.
The sentry chain, the powder cell, the link
Of pyramids of shot beside the shed,
Where bolstered steeds and troopers eat and drink.
The matches glow, a fuse for what's ahead,
A tindered wasteland waiting, hungry to be fed.

LII.

Yet he who leveled crowns with nodding head,
Pauses a moment, plays at god's delay;
The scourge is raised, not fallen. Soon the dead
Will choke the passes, soon the legions flay.
Spain, Spain! your vulture's shadow eats the day,
Its wings unfurled, its claws in crimson curled.
You'll reckon soon, when ruin makes its play,
When all your sons are scattered, flags unfurled,
And Hades takes the tithe it claims from this dumb world.

LIII.

And must they fall—the young, the unconsumed,
The firebrands fresh with music in their veins?
No step between submission and a tomb,
No middle ground but rapine and its chains?
Is valor mocked, is counsel drowned in pains,
Are zeal and fire and steel themselves in vain?
The god adored by man alone disdains
Their cries; he lets them perish, one by one,
And counts the bloodied dust as justice done.

LIV.

Was it for this the Spanish maid let fall
Her guitar's strings to snatch the soldier's knife?
She who once quailed at shadow, moth, or call,
Now stalks through corpses, hand in hand with strife.
Her voice is war's; her beauty brims with life.
She sings, she slays, she leads the sallying host.
And where her chief fell victim to the fife,
She fills his place, she makes the battle boast,
A girl whose gaze would make a Roman god a ghost.

LV.

And you who marvel—had you seen her then,
In softer hour, her veil of black aside,
Her hair more golden than the painter's pen,
Her eyes like blades, her laughter full of pride—
You'd never guess she dared the bayonet's stride.
Saragoza crowned her smile with blood and flame.
She thinned the ranks, she led the charge, defied,
And Glory—cheapened, battered, still the same—
Bent down and kissed her brow, and whispered her its name.

LVI.

Her lover dies; she sheds no widow's tear.
Her general falls; she takes his fatal post.
Her fellows flee; she checks them with her sneer.
The Gaul retreats, but she pursues the host.
Who else can feed the hungry lover's ghost?
Who else avenge the chieftain's fall so well?
She haunts the fleeing foe, their flight their cost,
Her hand the nightmare at their citadel,
The woman-warrior who made their courage quell.

LVII.

Yet Spain's dark daughters are no tribe of war,
But made for all the softer rites of love.
And if they march with men, it is not more
Than doves defending nests from hawks above.
Yet firmer far, their tenderness can shove
Aside the prating females, weak and wan.
Their charms are fierce, their passions clothed in glove,
Their minds more noble, fiercer than the spawn
Of lands where prattle rules, where beauty's thin and drawn.

LVIII.

Love's dimpled seal upon the cheek is proof
That softness reigns beneath the warrior's fire.
Her lips are pouts that bid a man stand proof,
Be valiant lest he lose the kiss's hire.
Her glance is flame that makes Apollo tire,
Her cheek unspoiled by Phoebus' heated lust.
What northern maid could claim a face entire?
How pale their forms, how weak their bodies, dust,
Beside this burning girl, this daughter fierce, robust.

LIX.

Compare them, poets, harems, what you please—
No paradise of Prophet's promised flame
Can match the dark-eyed Spanish girls at ease,
Who make of Heaven's throne a human frame.
Their kindled gaze, their angelic claim—
Outshines the Houris kept from mortal wind.
To them belongs the Prophet's lustrous name:
Black-eyed, angelic, sensuous, unconfined,
The Paradise of flesh the faithful long to find.

LX.

O Parnassus! I behold you now, awake,
Not dreamt in fable nor in painter's lie,
But reared in snow, in majesty that breaks
The shuddering heavens with your native sky.
What wonder if my feeble song should try?
The humblest pilgrim, stumbling on your road,
Would strum a string, would make a verse, a cry.
Though muses sleep, though none will now explode,
The silence still is loud where once the muses strode.

LXI.

I dreamed of you, O mountain, long ago.
Your name was glory, lore, divinest fame.
And now I stand before you, dumb, and know
My feeble verse dishonors such a name.
Your worshippers of old were crowned in flame;
I kneel instead, a beggar at your feet.
I dare not raise my voice, nor play the game,
But gaze, ashamed, beneath your cloudy seat,
And find in shameful joy the vision made complete.

LXII.

Yet happier I than those who never came,
The bards confined, who only dreamed your crest.
I see the spot, though Muses sleep in shame,
Though Apollo's cave lies cold, without a guest.
Yet still some spirit haunts the place, possessed,
That sighs in gale, that whispers in the cave.
It glides across the glassy stream, confessed,
A phantom teacher, hovering yet grave,
That lingers on the heights though gods forgot to save.

LXIII.

But let me turn, though trembling still with awe,
And bear away one relic of your site.
Some leaf of Daphne's plant, some sacred straw,
Some proof I passed beneath your holy height.
Spain's sons, Spain's daughters fade before my sight;
Forgive me, Muse, if briefly I betray—
But none who glimpsed you could withhold the rite.
I bent, I wept, I dared to pause and pray,
And left a votary's trace upon your path today.

LXIV.

Yet Greece, when young, did never circle round
Your slopes with brighter choir than Andaluz.
What maids are these? in beauty's lap they're crowned,
And soft desire burns hotter than the muse.
If only peace could bless them, they would choose
A gentler fate, a softer, finer stage.
As Greece still offers shade for love's abuse,
Though glory fled, though war erased her page,
So Spain deserved the peace denied her by her age.

LXV.

Proud Seville boasts her strength, her gilded days,
Her riches, ancient pride, her site and towers.
But Cadiz, by the coast, more sweetly sways—
Though steeped in vice, her praise is still of powers.
O Vice! how soft your pathways, how your flowers
Entangle youth, how magic is your stare.
Hydra-cherub, sprouting heads and bowers,
You shift, you mould, you take each mask you wear,
And men embrace the chains you whisper as a prayer.

LXVI.

When Paphos fell, O Time, your curse prevailed.
Venus herself abandoned home and hearth.
Yet constant to the sea from which she sailed,
She fled, she flew, she sought a second birth.
She made her shrine in Cadiz, made the earth
A temple, domes of white, a thousand strong.
And though no single church could house her mirth,
Her altars blaze with incense, wine, and song,
A liturgy of lust that holds the city long.

LXVII.

From dusk to dawn, from dawn to drunken dusk,
The revel rolls, the garlands choke the air.
The monks burn incense, thick, narcotic musk,
The lovers pray, the lovers praise despair.
Devices, frolics, fancies—all are there;
The sober joy is banished, chased away.
The riot reigns, the candles flare, beware:
Devotion kneels beside desire's bouquet,
And prayer itself is lust, and lust itself will pray.

LXVIII.

The Sabbath dawns, a holy rest in name;
But Cadiz makes it sacred to the beast.
The forest's monarch bellows, blood aflame,
He tramples steed and rider at the feast.
The crowd exults, demands the gore increased;
The women shriek for more, but not in grief.
The entrails spill, the bull becomes the priest,
And Death, parading, gives the day's relief,
A holiday of gore, the Holy Day of Thief.

LXIX.

The Sabbath here, in London's bloated sprawl,
Is not for prayer but spectacle of need;
Clerks, tailors, barbers, apprentices—all
Spill out in hacks and gigs with brutish speed.
To Hampstead, Brentford, Harrow, jades must bleed,
Till sweating nags collapse in foaming grime.
The mob exults, the churls deride the steed—
This weekly rite, a parody of time,
Profanes the holy day with commerce dressed as prime.

LXX.

Some row the Thames with ribboned girls in tow,
Some drive the turnpikes, some ascend the hill.
Some scud to Ware, to Richmond others go,
Some climb to Highgate, panting, drunk with will.
Why? Boeotian shades!—the Horn, the Horn to fill.
They drink, they dance, they consecrate their lust.
The oath is sworn, the horn is lifted still,
And mystery's name is whispered in the dust,
While night becomes their shrine, their god, their creed unjust.

LXXI.

Such sport the Spaniard calls a holy show,
The maid applauds, the swain exults in blood;
From youth he learns in vengeance' fire to glow,
To feast on pain, to gorge another's good.
The village, too, is thick with feud and feud,
Where neighbors plot for trifles, blow for blow.
The phalanx meets abroad in warlike mood,
Yet still at home, in darkness' afterglow,
A whispered knife repays the insult dealt below.

LXXII.

Gone are the locks, the bolts, duenna's gaze,
The dotard's rusted cage of jealousy.
The Spanish girl once roamed through summer's blaze,
Her tresses braided, bounding, loose, and free.
Ere war, that god of ash, had claimed the sea,
The night was lit by Venus, soft and green.
The dance was love's, the moon a canopy—
Now all is fire, volcanic rage obscene,
And innocence has fled where warlords intervene.

LXXIII.

And Harold too had loved, or thought he did—
For rapture is a dream, a rented mask.
But lately he had learned what joy kept hid:
Love's sweetest springs conceal a poisoned flask.
How fair, how young, how soft, the lips that ask—
Yet venom bubbles, bitter, from the core.
The smile is false, the gift a cruel task;
The fount of bliss is brackish evermore,
A festival of loss behind a gilded door.

LXXIV.

Yet beauty still he saw, though passion slept;
No philosophic calm had stilled his eyes.
But Vice had dug his grave, and Pleasure crept
To bury hope, to whisper all was lies.
He walked with Gloom, beneath Cain's branded skies,
Life's victim, weary, hollowed, restless, cursed.
The mark was his, the doom he could not prize,
And even Beauty's balm, its charm rehearsed,
Could never cure the soul that damned itself the first.

LXXV.

Still he beheld, but mingled not, apart.
He would have joined the song, the dance, the fair,
But who can smile with ruin in his heart?
No pleasure pierced the shroud of his despair.
Yet once he struggled, breathing Beauty's air,
And in her bower, pensive, strained to sing.
He poured unstudied music, bleak but rare,
A lay untrimmed, a raw unpolished thing,
Addressed to Inez' charms, his lost imagining.

1.

Smile not at this, my sullen-bastard brow;
No smile remains—Botoxed, embalmed, erased.
May Heaven spare thee tears that stain the now,
Though mine are inkless, scrawled on walls defaced.
My joy is cancer, metastasized, misplaced;
Thy eyes would drown in pity's rotted brine.
And if thou weep, the weeping is debased—
I wear a mask, the face no longer mine,
And mourn a ghost within, the crime without a sign.

2.

Thou askest what disease corrodes my youth,
What cancer gnaws the marrow of my days.
The pang is nameless, crueler than truth;
A wound that bleeds in silence, not in praise.
It is the whisper heard in mirrored haze,
The secret grief that fame cannot redeem.
Not even thou could soothe, in all thy ways;
Thy hand might touch, but touch becomes a dream,
And all thy balm dissolves, a needle in the stream.

3.

It is not love, though love once scorched my bed;
Nor hatred, though I burn at what is lost.
It is not crowns of power on my head,
Nor ambition's baubles counted, weighed, and tossed.
All these I fled, and none repaid the cost.
It is the rot of pleasures drained and done.
The gala ended, credits rolled, and crossed—
And still the horror dawns with every sun,
The knowledge nothing's left, the script cannot be spun.

4.

From every sight, from every word, it springs,
This weariness, this plague without a cure.
No pleasure heals, no beauty even stings;
Thy eyes, once spells, are vacant, insecure.
Thy gaze, though holy, cannot now ensure
A spark of life, for even love's a fraud.
I scroll and scroll, the void becomes obscure;
A click, a swipe, the meme that masks the clod,
The screen that eats the soul, the algorithm god.

5.

This ceaseless gloom, this ceaseless exile's curse,
I bear like Cain, with mark upon my face.
No rest before the tomb, no blessing terse,
No promise made of sleep, no gift of grace.
The wanderer drags his shadow through each place,
And will not hope, and cannot even die.
The sun is lead, the moon a cheap disgrace.
I dream of graves, but graves will yet deny,
And even death withholds, and even worms pass by.

6.

Exile from self—what exile could be more?
To flee from city, desert, sea, and sky,
Yet drag the self, that parasite, ashore,
The voice that whispers, mocks, and will not die.
I flee to Rome, to Delphi, yet the lie
Pursues, the blight remains, the thought returns.
No ocean drowns, no mountain sanctifies;
I run to death, yet every death adjourns—
The demon thought persists, the soul within still burns.

7.

Yet others dance, as if the night were kind,
As if the dream were true, the song not fake.
Their laughter drowns the darkness from their mind;
Their joy is counterfeit I cannot break.
Oh, may they sleep, and never once awake;
Let pleasure drug them, let their slumber stay.
For waking is the curse I cannot shake;
Their dream is mercy, mine the break of day,
Where everything is ash, and love is swept away.

8.

Through many lands my pilgrimage is cast,
And retrospection is my only guest.
The curse of memory brands me to the last;
The worst I know, and knowing, find my rest.
The worst has been, and worse cannot molest.
The ruin's done, the embers will not flame.
What solace left but this: I've stood the test,
I've drunk the gall, I've borne the weight of shame,
And tasted hell alive, and known it by its name.

9.

And what that worst? I dare not let thee see;
Compassion's gaze would falter, pity tear.
Smile on—remain untouched by misery,
For knowledge is the wound thou must not bear.
To peel the mask is to reveal the snare—
The heart's abyss, the pit, the inner tomb.
If thou didst look, thou wouldst be broken there,
For man's true heart is only hell and gloom,
A coffin nailed in flesh, a living soul's dark room.

LXXVI.

Adieu, fair Cadiz! long adieu, at last!
You stood unbroken while the world decayed;
When all were bought, betrayed, or overcast,
You first were free, and last to be dismayed.
Though traitor's blood your streets at times displayed,
It was the traitor only came to fall.
Your nobles—false; your people, unafraid.
The Conqueror's chain was hugged by none at all,
Save knaves in robes of rank, save chivalry's recall.

LXXVII.

Such is Spain: her fate a paradox,
Her people free in bondage, proud in chains.
Her chiefs betray, her vassals face the shocks;
Her slaves are true, her nobles steeped in stains.
Her land is loved, though love repays with pains.
Back to the knife, the war, the endless strife!
The cry is "War!" though war the foe sustains.
They fight for liberty, not liberty of life—
A freedom mocked, betrayed, yet worshipped as their wife.

LXXVIII.

Would you know Spain? Then read her book of gore,
Her annals penned in dagger, flame, and shot.
From flashing sabres to the secret sore,
Each weapon serves the cause, dishonored not.
The husband strikes, the brother, unforgot,
The sister's honor, wife's revenge, their plea.
The oppressor bleeds, the tyrant's back is hot,
The foe is butchered—such their legacy:
The most remorseless deed their creed of liberty.

LXXIX.

Pity the dead? Then walk the reeking plain,
See entrails steaming in the vulture's sun.
The hands of women clothed in murder's stain,
The corpses left unburied, carrion.
The bones bleached white, the gore that will not run,
Remain as monuments of human awe.
The fields are sermons preached to everyone,
That sons may learn, when memory is raw,
The hideous truth of war that laughs at mortal law.

LXXX.

And still it deepens—Pyrenean gorges
Spill forth new legions, endless, iron, blind.
The work is barely started; doom disgorges
The maw of nations chained and undermined.
Strange fate—that Spain, by blood so redefined,
Should free the worlds her greed once made a slave.
Columbia breathes, her shackles left behind,
Though Quito's sons lie buried in the grave,
And Murder prowls at home, unmastered, fierce, depraved.

LXXXI.

Not Talavera's carnage, nor the spume
Of Barossa's slaughter, nor the heap
Of Albuera's butcheries of doom
Could win the peace that Spain still longs to keep.
The olive branch is withered in her sleep.
How many nights must swallow doubtful days
Before the robber turns, the spoilers weep,
And Freedom's alien tree takes root and stays,
A native growth at last, not grafted by a blaze?

LXXXII.

And thou, my friend!—I bleed to think of thee,
Not fallen crowned with laurel in the fight.
Had death been glory, pride could bend the knee,
And Friendship would have borne the cruel rite.
But thus to fade, unlaurelled, out of sight,
Forgotten save by one forsaken heart,
Unreckoned in the tally of the night,
While meaner men in gaudy triumph start—
That was thy fate, to rot unpraised, to stand apart.

LXXXIII.

Oh, earliest known, and dearest, lost to me!
In hopeless days, thou wert my last and best.
Though gone for ever, in my dreams I see
Thy form return, though morning breaks the rest.
The tear renews, though never confessed,
Till I too sink to join thee where thou art.
One bier shall bind the mourner to the blessed,
One grave unite the severed, torn apart,
Till dust and dust embrace, one grief, one heart.

LXXXIV.

So ends this fytte of Harold's pilgrimage.
The critic sneers—"too much!"—but let him wait.
The pilgrim's tale is writ on Nature's page,
And I, a scribbler, merely scrawl at fate.
Patience! More lands, more ruins yet await,
Where Eld still lingers, monuments remain,
Where Greece stood proud before barbaric hate,
Before her glories perished, yet in vain—
There Harold roams, and I must follow with my strain.

Canto the Second

I.

Come, Botoxed Maid of Heaven!—but thou, alas,
Didst never ghost a mortal's screen-time scroll;
The Goddess once had temples built of glass,
Now franchise gyms and juice bars mark the whole.
War's Instagram, Time's ash, and Fame's black hole
Seem kinder than the rule of men who brand
Their TEDx glow across the mortal soul,
And never felt the sacred fever's hand—
The platinum thought that burns, yet few can understand.

II.

Ancient Athena, Botoxed mother—where,
Where are the men of myth, the grandees bold?
Gone—ghosting through the pixelated air:
A Netflix pitch, a story optioned, sold,
First in the race for laurels, streamed, then cold.
A schoolboy's tale, forgotten after lunch!
The warrior's weapon, sophist's thread of gold,
Are searched in vain among the ruins' crunch—
Gray flits the shade of power, mocked by the tourist bunch.

III.

O Morning's Son, rise! only do not touch
Yon urn, defenseless prop in a soundstage lot.
Behold this sepulcher, nation's ruin, much
Like a shuttered mall where gods have lost their plot.
Faith franchises, each fad replaces what
The last one hawked; Jove, Mahomet, now brand-
New gurus trending—incense fades to rot.
The child of Doubt, of Death, in feed-scroll's sand,
Hope built on clickbait reeds, no altar to withstand.

IV.

Chained to the Earth, he lifts his eyes to sky—
Is it not curse enough that he must be?
Why beg a sequel, clueless where or why,
Content to sign the waiver sight unseen?
A package deal: you're merged with air, with screen,
In heaven's pilot season, casting wide.
Still dreaming joy and horror, post-machine;
Weigh that gray dust before it drifts aside:
This little urn speaks more than sermons sanctified.

V.

Unseal the mound where vanished heroes sleep;
Far on the beach their ghostly credits roll.
He fell, a nation's extras queued to weep,
Now not one fan remains to play the role,
No warlike vigil staged, no shrine patrol.
Remove that skull from out the rubble's pile:
Is this a temple fit to house a soul?
The worm itself, bored with its set-design style,
Disdains the shattered cell, unworthy to beguile.

VI.

Gaze on the broken arch, the tagged-up wall,
The chambers desolate, the portals foul.
Yes, once Ambition held her casting call,
The Dome of Thought, the Palace of the Soul.
Behold through eyeless sockets, blank and dull,
The gilded rooms where wisdom pitched its wit,
Where passions staged their tantrums, lost control.
Can saint or sophist, script or gospel writ,
Repeople this dead tower, reboot what's counterfeit?

VII.

Well said, Athena's sharpest native son:
"All that we know is, nothing can be known."
Why tremble at what cannot be outrun?
Each life its pang, yet dreamers make their own,
Conjuring Netflix evils in the bone.
Go chase what Fate or ratings deign to bless;
Peace waits us on that shore where silence's grown.
There's no forced banquet, no influencer's mess:
Rest spreads her couch, eternal, endless, bodiless.

VIII.

Yet if, as holiest pundits swore, there be
A land of souls beyond the black-walled screen,
To shame the Sadducee's philosophy,
The sophists vain with TED-talks, half-obscene,
How sweet to binge old episodes, once seen,
And hear those voices canceled from the light!
To stream the shades whose work made labors lean,
The Samian sage, the Bactrian's ghost recite,
And all who taught the Right appear in Dolby bright.

IX.

There Thou!—whose love and life at once were cut,
Left me to live and love in vain, in debt.
Twined with my heart, can I believe the shut
Of death is final, when your flashbulbs set
Still blind me nightly? No, I'll dream we met,
Woo visions to my vacant streaming chest;
If young remembrance in the code be set,
Let future's algorithm judge the rest:
For me 'tis bliss enough to know thy spirit blest.

X.

Here let me sit upon this slab of stone,
The marble column's still-intact base.
Here, Saturn's son, thou hadst thy favorite throne,
Mightiest of many, vanished without trace.
The grandeur latent haunts the dwelling-place,
But Fancy's CGI cannot restore.
These pillars claim no sigh, no tourist's grace;
The Moslem sits unmoved, the Greek sings more,
Light carols drifting by the ruin's shattered door.

XI.

But who among the plunderers of that fane—
Where Pallas lingered, loth to leave her reign—
Was worst? the final spoiler, smug and plain.
Blush, Caledonia! He bore thy name.
England, rejoice—no child of thine the shame!
Thy free-born men should spare what once was free;
Yet still they shipped the relics, all the same,
Hearing the altars moan across the sea,
Their sighs packed up in crates for London's gallery.

XII.

The modern Pict's ignoble boast: to tear
What Goth, what Turk, what centuries had spared.
Cold as the cliffs of his own northern air,
Barren his mind, his heart a stone declared.
He planned, prepared, displaced what Time had cared.
Athena's children, weak to guard the shrine,
Still felt their mother's wound, her sorrow shared.
They never knew till then the iron line
Of despot's chain, engraved with British seal and sign.

XIII.

What! shall the British tongue once dare to say
Albion was glad in Athens' bitter tears?
Though in thy name the tyrants had their way,
Tell not the deed to Europe, lest she hears.
The ocean queen, Britannia through the years,
Who once gave aid, now snatches at the brand—
Tears down the relics, mocks what Greece reveres,
Rips marble from the earth with harpy's hand,
What tyrants spared she stole, and Eld could barely stand.

XIV.

Where was thine Ægis, Pallas, once that scared
The Goths, stern Alaric, havoc on their ride?
Where Peleus' son, whose shade from Hades flared,
Burst into light, in armor, death-supplied?
What, could not Pluto spare him, once, to guide,
To guard a second time the city's bones?
Idly he wandered, pacing Stygian tide,
Nor came to scare away the looters' drones,
And walls he loved collapsed, abandoned to the stones.

XV.

Cold is the heart, fair Greece, that looks on thee,
And feels not like a lover at the tomb;
Dull is the eye that will not weep to see
Thy shrines demolished, thy proud halls consumed,
By British hands, whose mission was presumed
To guard what relics never can be made.
Curst be the hour those sails abroad resumed,
And once again thy breast was torn, betrayed,
Thy shrinking gods removed, in foreign ice displayed.

XVI.

But where is Harold? Must I now forget
To prod the gloomy wanderer on his way?
Little he cared for all that men regret;
No fake lament from friends could make him stay.
No hand to clasp, no tear to shed, to say
Farewell—the stranger sailed for other climes.
His heart was hard, immune to charm's cliché;
Yet Harold felt not as in former times,
And left without a sigh the land of war and crimes.

XVII.

He who has sailed upon the blue-screen sea
Has seen at times a vision bright and rare:
The sails white-set, the gallant frigate free,
The masts and spires retreating, fading there.
The glorious main expanding, wide and bare,
The convoy spread like swans against the sky.
The dullest sailor boldened in the air,
So gaily curled the waves, the prows danced high—
The spectacle itself was pure commodity.

XVIII.

And oh, the little warlike world within!
The guns well-reeved, the canopy well-strung,
The hoarse command, the bustling human din,
When at a word the sailors climbed and clung.
Hark, the boatswain's call, the cheering sung!
The rope slides quick through every seaman's hand;
The midship boy, shrill-voiced, unbroken-lunged,
Blows pipe and guides the men to Fate's demand—
An urchin's whistle leads the laboring band.

XIX.

White was the glassy deck, unstained, precise,
Where staid lieutenants walked the watchful round;
A sacred space was marked for sacrifice:
The lone commander, feared yet seldom found,
Stalked silent, lest his gravity unbound.
So must he keep restraint, nor mingle much;
That barrier once dissolved, his fame was drowned.
Yet Britons rarely swerve, however such:
They law their lives, and nerve their strength by duty's clutch.

XX.

Blow, swiftly blow, thou gale compelling keel,
Till broad-eyed sun withdraws his lessening ray!
Then must the pennant-bearer slacken feel,
That slower hulks might crawl along the way.
A grievance sore, a dull delay, to stay
And waste the sweetest breeze on laggard craft.
What leagues are lost before the break of day!
Thus loitering pensive on the willing draft,
The flapping sails hauled down, for ships adrift and daft.

XXI.

The moon's a klieg, and heaven's a rented lot,
Her spotlight strafes the tar on ocean's face;
The extras on the pier rehearse their plot,
Believing they are loved, rehearsing grace.
A Bluetooth Orpheus beats time, his bass
Snared in the throats of vape-lit revelers near;
They move as if the rave could still erase
The fact that bailiffs dog their rented cheer—
Till dawn dissolves their lease, twelve beats too late to hear.

XXII.

Through straits of glass-and-chrome I watch the coasts:
Two continents of strip malls locked in stare;
Dark-eyed divorcées scroll, their Botox hosts,
While shadow apps patrol the midnight air.
On Spain's soft shore, the god-light makes it fair—
Revealing rust, a franchise, forest brown;
But Africa's skyscrapers snarl and glare,
Their blackout teeth descending through the town,
Till freeway cliffs collapse and pour their poison down.

XXIII.

It's night, when every feed insists we feel
We once were touched—though love's a brand recall;
The heart, last mourner at the endless reel,
Rewinds the ghost of friends who blocked us all.
Who bends beneath the years, once glam and tall,
When youth itself survives the failed deploy?
What meme, what clip, what like can still enthrall,
When mingling souls no longer blend to joy?—
Then death's just click-off mode: one more forgotten toy.

XXIV.

Bent over yacht-rails, peering at the screen,
The soul forgets her startup IPO;
Her hope-decked pitch decks vanish, all unseen,
Her pride dissolves in childhood's after-glow.
Yet even trolls confess, in private woe,
That something once was dear, possessed, possessed—
A hashtag buried deep, too far to show.
The sudden pang arrives, the heavy chest
Would shed its weight of grief, but fails at each request.

XXV.

To squat on rocks, to scroll through feeds of hell,
To wander streets where ghosts of brands convene,
Where things beyond the franchise choose to dwell,
And Man's dominion flickers on a screen;
To climb the stairwell, rooftop, mezzanine,
With flocks of drones that never need a home;
Alone above the traffic's tortured sheen,
You lean on towers, lit by data's foam—
Not solitude, but nature's showroom, endless Chrome.

XXVI.

But in the swarm, the pixel-surge of men,
To hear, to see, to touch, and never bless,
And drift the malls, a captive citizen,
With no one smiling, no one to confess;
Assistants ghost you, stylists won't caress,
And Splendor's minions flee from bankrupt cries;
No kindred stream, no tender consciousness
Would notice if your avatar just dies—
This is alone: the room's alive with ringlight lies.

XXVII.

More blest the hermit, god of Athos wild,
Whose live-stream climbs a cliff-face for the view;
At dusk he watches filters turn things mild,
The sea remade in cyan, skies in blue.
He lingers, knowing that the hour is true—
A holy frame, a still unbranded shot;
Then slowly clicks away, as watchers do,
And sighs: "What if this life had been my lot?"
Then hates the world he left, a gig he half forgot.

XXVIII.

So pass the circuits, flights, the endless track,
The noise that leaves no echo in the mind;
So pass the storms, the spin, the market's hack,
The fickle gusts of trending, fast-rewind;
So pass the joys and sorrows, blind on blind,
Cooped in a penthouse, Wi-Fi's citadel;
The foul—the fair—the fail—the sudden kind—
As breezes crash, as bills and credits swell,
Till morning's breaking news: land ho, and all is well.

XXIX.

Yet don't in silence skip Calypso's isles,
Those influencers adrift in middle deep;
For there the weary scroll, though false their smiles,
And goddess streams her tears no more to keep.
She waits for him who chose a mortal cheap—
For likes that fade, for coins that never ride;
Her boy attempted mentor's ghastly leap,
The coach had urged him, plummeting with pride;
So double loss she bore, and doubly sighed.

XXX.

Her reign is gone, her gentle glories dead:
But youth, beware, for danger stalks the throne.
A sovereign mortal rules the feed instead,
And you may find Calypso in your phone.
Sweet Florence, had I courage of my own,
This wayward heart might dare to claim it thine;
But shackled here, I drop no worthless stone,
Nor dare to bid that breast one pang of mine—
Better to ghost than risk contagion of decline.

XXXI.

Thus Harold thought, as in that Lady's eyes
He saw a light—no thought, no tethered plot,
Save admiration, flickering as it dies;
Love stood aloof, a rumor half forgot.
The godling knew his votary was caught
Too many times, but now would kneel no more;
No Cupid arrow sang, no fever shot;
He'd closed the app, the boyhood rites were o'er—
The god dismissed his sway, one brand to shop no more.

XXXII.

Fair Florence found, with something like dismay,
A man unmoved by her rehearsed command;
For every gaze was trained to weep, to sway,
And worship Beauty's weapon, close at hand.
They wept, they moaned, they kissed her PayPal brand,
Her law, her lash, her punishment, her flame;
But he, raw youth, withstood her gaze so grand,
And never joined the worshippers in shame—
A marvel that no fire had set his heart aflame.

XXXIII.

She did not know that heart of concrete mask,
That silence, pride, the spoiled marauder's game;
His snares were spread, his conquests just a task,
And still he stalked for quarry worth the name.
But Harold would no longer play that claim;
The spoil was worthless, games no more employed.
And had he swooned for those blue eyes the same,
He never would have joined that whining void—
That lovers' cult of tears, a pastime to avoid.

XXXIV.

He little knows of Woman's breast, I ween,
Who thinks that sighs will tilt the scales of lust;
What careth she for hearts, once trapped and seen?
Do homage to the eyes, but not too just;
Too humble, and she'll grind your suit to dust.
So mask your tenderness, if you are wise;
For Confidence, the brisk, will earn her trust,
While Pique and soothe in turn will mesmerize—
Till Passion crowns your head, and every rule denies.

XXXV.

It's an old lesson—Time repeats the lie,
And those who know it curse its bitter ghost;
When all is won that all desire to buy,
The prize is paltry, hardly worth the cost.
Youth wasted, honor tarnished, mind engrossed;
These are your fruits, successful Passion's creed.
If Hope is strangled, kindly cruel and lost,
It festers still, a never-healing need,
A sickness love forgets, but leaves the wound to bleed.

XXXVI.

Away! I cannot loiter in this song;
The feed demands we scroll a thousand more,
And many landscapes wait, both weak and strong,
By sadness guided, not by fable's lore.
Climes fairer than a mortal mind can store,
Unspooling utopias none can keep;
Imagined heavens, fabricated score,
That teach what man could be—but never reap,
If ever man were taught beyond corruption's sleep.

XXXVII.

Dear Nature, Mother streaming always still!
Though filtered, shifting, mild in every frame;
From her bare breast I take my endless fill,
Her never-weaned, though not her favored claim.
Oh, she is fairest when she's fierce and lame,
When wildness glares, and polish slinks away;
By day or night she plays her changeless game,
Though few will see her stripped of app's array—
I've sought her most in wrath, and loved her most that way.

XXXVIII.

Land of Albania! where the warrior rose,
A theme for youth, a warning for the sage;
And he, his namesake, baffling countless foes,
Whose tales light up the classroom's faded stage.
O land of rugged nurse and savage rage,
Where cross and crescent flash in shifting skies!
The minarets ignite, the priests engage,
The pale half-moon in every cypress lies—
Each city groves its faith, its glimmered compromise.

XXXIX.

Childe Harold sailed, and passed Penelope's pain,
The widow scanning waves for faithless shore;
He glimpsed the mount where lovers fled in vain,
And Sappho's grave, her fire alive no more.
Dark Sappho—verse could not your flesh restore,
Though ink immortal scorched your lines with flame;
Could she not live who life eternal bore?
If any afterworld awaits a name,
It waits the lyric ghost that Heaven dares not claim.

XL

It was a Grecian autumn, soft and sly,
When Harold hailed Leucadia's cape from far;
He longed to see it, lingered for its sky,
But marked with scorn the remnants left by war:
Actium, Lepanto, Trafalgar's scar.
He watched unmoved, for he despised the fight—
Born under some inglorious, nameless star,
He loathed the trade of bravos, martial blight,
And laughed at soldier's dreams, a bored civilian wight.

XLI.

The evening star was trending, lit above
Leucadia's jagged promontory of grief;
A backdrop built for dramas sold as love,
Where falling bodies blur in disbelief.
The yacht slid slow, beneath that cliff of brief
Romance—its billows made a dirge below.
And Harold's gaze, long drained by click and leaf,
Seemed smooth at last, as if his face could show
A peace no serum sells, nor any app can know.

XLII.

Then dawn: Albania's hills, stern firewall,
Dark peaks of Suli, Pindus' jagged crown;
Half-draped in mist, with rivulets that fall,
Purpled with streaks, a glitching royal gown.
The clouds break loose—the mountaineers look down,
Their eyes as sharp as wolves, their breath of knives;
Here eagles preen, here predators renown
Their savagery, while storm-front still contrives
To shake the year apart, convulsing shattered lives.

XLIII.

Now Harold felt himself at last unmoored,
And left behind the tongues that shaped his youth;
He touched a shore admired but still abhorred,
The land of strangers, radiant, raw with truth.
His breast was steeled, his needs were bare and smooth;
He sought no peril, yet he did not flee;
The savage scene, refreshed by ceaseless ruth,
Turned toil to nectar, gave him currency—
In winter's scourge he burned, in summer's heat was free.

XLIV.

Here the red Cross remains, a rusted brand,
Scoffed by the circumcised with side-eye sneer;
It once adorned the priests with holy hand,
Now Votaries and Church alike appear
As hustlers in the bazaar of faith and fear.
Foul Superstition—mask for every creed!
Your idols change, your symbols interchange,
But profit's altar feeds on every need—
A sacral Ponzi scheme, where worship dies of greed.

XLV.

Behold Ambracia's gulf, where once was spilled
A world for Woman—harmless, doomed delight;
In rippling bay, the hosts of empires filled
With blood and brass, a slaughter staged for spite.
The second Caesar's trophies touched the height,
And withered now, like hands that raised them high.
Imperial Anarchs doubled human blight;
Was Earth ordained, O God, to satisfy
The porn of endless win-and-lose beneath your sky?

XLVI.

From borders rough to Illyria's valley floor,
Childe Harold passed through mountains rarely named;
Scarce noted in the footnotes of old lore,
Yet lovelier than the lands the poets framed.
Not Tempe, not Parnassus—famed, proclaimed—
Could match the secret dales this coast concealed.
Though Attic soil with sacred myths was shamed,
The unnamed valleys flaunt their unsealed yield,
Outstripping classic ground, where fame itself congealed.

XLVII.

He passed bleak Pindus, lake Acherusia grim,
And left the primal city in its dust;
Onward he journeyed, drawn to spectres dim,
To greet Albania's Chief, a lord of lust.
Lawless law was his—obedience or bust;
His bloody hand reigned turbulent and bold.
Yet mountain-bands in crags, unbent by trust,
Defied his power, hurled defiance cold—
They bowed to gold alone, their freedom bought, not sold.

XLVIII.

Monastic Zitza—favoured holy ground,
Your brow a rainbow dome of tinted air;
Where rock and torrent, forest, sky resound,
And cataracts baptize the pilgrims there.
Each painted charm, each mountain's lifted stare,
Enfolds the gazer in its vast caress.
The torrent's rushing, music of despair,
Between the hanging rocks in wild excess—
A shock that pleases still, sublime in harsh finesse.

XLIX.

Amidst the grove that crowns the tufted hill,
Where convent walls in chalk-white armor gleam,
The caloyer abides—no heart of chill,
But hospitable, warm as ancient dream.
The passer is received, not turned to stream;
No niggard host, no petty scorn is here.
The mountains throng, the peaks in chorus teem,
And one may linger, free of urban sneer,
To drink of Nature's sheen and feel her presence clear.

L.

Here in the sultriest hour, the pilgrim lies,
Beneath the trees that whisper cool reprieve;
The winds of Heaven fan his weary sighs,
And breezes bless the breast that dares believe.
Far down, the plain lies scorched, a choking sieve;
But here the air is clean, the day benign.
Disease can't climb, its breath cannot deceive;
So let him rest, where heaven and forest twine,
And gaze at morn, at noon, at eve, in calm divine.

LI.

Then dusky, huge, the Alps Chimæra spread,
A volcanic amphitheatre of dread;
Below, the valley stirred, alive not dead,
With flocks and trees and rivers spirit-fed.
The mountain firs bent low, the torrent bled;
And Acheron, black witness to the tomb,
Still flowed where Pluto's worship once was said.
If this be Hell, then close Elysium's room—
No other heaven I seek, no after-death perfume.

LII.

No city's towers corrupt this honest view;
Though Yanina lies hidden, veiled in haze.
Here men are scarce, the hamlets thin and few,
The shepherd scarce appears beneath the blaze.
The goats cling perilous on cliff-bound maze,
And pensive, draped in white capote, the boy
Leans on his rock and watches storm displays,
Or waits in cave as thunder's short-lived toy,
A witness small to fate, to ruin, to alloy.

LIII.

Where now, Dodona, is your ancient grove,
The oracle, the fount of Jupiter?
No whisper left, no shrine remains to prove,
No thunder's echo shakes the valley bare.
Forgotten all—and Man would still despair
That his own tether, frail, must break at last?
Fool, see the fate of Gods: their idols wear.
Would you outlive the marble and the past,
When tongues and nations sink, their monuments downcast?

LIV.

Epirus fades, its mountains bow to plain;
The weary eye descends with glad relief.
And smoothest vales, in spring's resplendent chain,
Are robed in grass, in blossoms, bright though brief.
A river cuts the calm, defies the grief,
Its banks with woods that wave and shadows play;
Their glassy twins below reflect belief,
Or with the moonlight sleep in midnight's sway—
A solemn trance that veils the landscape's brief decay.

LV.

The sun dropped low, behind vast Tomerit's height;
The Laos roared, a river fierce, unkind.
The shades of night were closing fast with blight,
When Harold, winding banks, at last divined
The glittering towers of Tepalen aligned.
Like meteors, minarets inflamed the sky;
The busy hum of warriors filled his mind,
The campfires bristled, swords were lifted high—
The breeze bore soldier-songs, the death-songs of supply.

LVI.

He passed beneath the Haram's silent tower,
And through the arch where Despots make their seat;
A palace there, and fort in one dark flower,
Where eunuchs, soldiers, slaves in fever meet.
The pomp was common, yet obscene, complete;
The Despot on his dais, coldly crowned.
Preparations shook the court with fevered feet;
The santons, guests, the drummers drummed the ground—
A Babel of the world, where every creed was found.

LVII.

The horses glittered, saddled for parade,
And weapons glistened, hoarded for the war.
Above, the corridors with factions swayed,
Each tribe adorned, each color's lore.
And through the echoing gates there rushed once more
A Tartar spurring steed to vanish fast;
The Turk, the Greek, the Moor, the Albanian bore
Their hues, their tongues, their hatreds unsurpassed,
While drums announced the night, the day of war at last.

LVIII.

The wild Albanian, kirtled at the knee,
His shawl-bound head, his rifle wrought with art;
The Macedonian, crimson-scarfed and free;
The Delhi, cap of terror to impart;
The supple Greek, a mimic in the mart;
The Nubian slave, disfigured, mutilate;
The Turk, too proud to speak, too cold of heart,
His beard a flag, his silence fit for state—
These mingled tribes parade, their difference to elate.

LIX.

Some recline in conspiracies of ease,
Surveying motley markets of the court;
Some bow in prayer, their murmurs on the breeze;
Some smoke, some gamble, each in base resort.
The Albanian struts, the Greek's sly words consort,
While from the mosque the muezzin's voice ascends:
The call to prayer, the solemn, stark report,
Shakes minarets, each echo loud portends—
"There is no God but God!" the night to silence bends.

LX.

And now Ramazani's fast was near its close;
The day's long penance lifted at twilight.
Then feast, then revel—every chamber knows
The menial train prepares for festal rite.
The galleries rang, each room a furnace bright,
As slaves and pages shuffled food within.
The mingling din of board and feast ignite;
The chambers teemed, the corridors grew thin,
As guests devoured the night, and drank of worldly sin.

LXI.

Here woman's voice is muted, veiled from air,
Her body signed away, her heart on lease;
She yields to one, and calls submission care,
Her cage recast as sanctuary, peace.
The Master loves—so what? The leases cease
To honor self, replaced by child's demand.
And motherhood's narcotic brings release,
Her babe the breast commands with holy hand—
No meaner passion lives, no other will withstand.

LXII.

A marble hall, a fountain burbling still,
A couch where silk exhales its scented breath;
Here Ali lounged—a monument of will,
A man of wars and debts and casual death.
His face, benign, as if no hell beneath;
A mask of gentleness, a smile of years;
But every line concealed a beast unsheathed,
A legacy of blood, of rapine's tears—
The portrait sits serene, while carnage disappears.

LXIII.

It is not age that drapes his beard in frost,
For Hafiz sang of love that conquers time;
Nor youth alone, by passion seized and lost,
Can claim the ruin of his storied crime.
The tooth of tigers leaves its perfect rhyme;
The man who starts in blood will end in blood.
So Ali moved, a relic past his prime,
Whose hand, once smeared, returned to scarlet flood—
Till age itself seemed drunk, still drunk on human mud.

LXIV.

The Pilgrim rested here, his senses torn
By carpets, courtyards, perfumes thick with ease;
A palace built to hush the city's horn,
A hideout for the Grandeur's sated disease.
Such wealth, such wantonness, such toys to please,
Yet quickly wearied him, their charms a snare.
Peace hates the staged repose of tapestries;
Pleasure with Pomp is poison in the air,
Their marriage breeds disgust, their union breeds despair.

LXV.

Fierce sons of Albania—virtues raw,
Untutored yet, but written in their veins;
No foe has ever seen their backs withdraw,
They bear the wars, they sing beneath their pains.
Their mountains guard them more than iron chains;
Their wrath is fatal, but their faith is true.
When Gratitude or Valour stakes its claims,
They rush unshaken, storming into view—
Wherever Chief may lead, they bleed because they do.

LXVI.

Childe Harold saw them thronging, fierce and proud,
The tower alight with splendor and with guile;
And later saw them, when the fates allowed
Him captive to distress, himself reviled.
That hour, when men turn hot and hatred wild,
These warriors gave him shelter, roof, and bread.
Barbarians less would never be so mild,
While kin at home had scorned, or turned and fled—
Few hearts withstand the test when hatred wants you dead.

LXVII.

It happened once his bark was driven hard
On Suli's coast, a shore of ragged stone;
The night was desolate, the stars were barred,
The sea hissed warnings, dark, obscene, alone.
To land was peril, but to sail was blown;
The sailors doubted, sniffed for traitor's spoor.
At last they touched the rocks with trembling moan,
Half-fearing Suli's sons, who hate the poor—
The Frank, the Turk alike, each butchered as before.

LXVIII.

Vain fears! The Suliotes stretched out their hands,
And led the strangers through the swamp and shale;
Their hearth was built, their wine unstopped, their brands
Burned clothes to warmth, their cheer refused to fail.
No polish here, no salon's painted tale,
But kindness real, however rough the deed.
Philanthropy, so rare in gilded pale,
Shone brighter here than courts of crassly bred—
They fed the hungry heart, they soothed the soul in need.

LXIX.

It came to pass, marauders blocked his road,
And left Acarnania wrapped in brand and blade;
So Harold chose a band to share his load,
Men seasoned well, with war and labor made.
Together through the forests dark they strayed,
Till Achelous' stream at last they found.
Its banks were white, its tide a mirror laid;
And further still, Ætolia's hills rose round—
The journey wide with blood, the journey cursed with sound.

LXX.

Where Utraikey forms its secret cove,
And weary waves recline in silver rest,
The hills lean down, their foliage dark above,
Nodding at midnight on the bay's soft breast.
The western winds, like whispered ghosts, caressed
The water's face, but ruffled not its frame.
Here Harold came, received a gentle guest;
And from the Night drew joys too pure to name,
Soft solace gathered here, though nothing stayed the same.

LXXI.

The shore was ringed with fire, the feast was done,
The red wine circled, faces burned with light;
An uninvited watcher would have run,
So strange the pageant breaking through the night.
At midnight's stillest pulse began the rite:
The Palikars unsheathed, then cast away,
Their sabres clanged, they joined their hands in flight,
And bound in circle, man to man, they swayed—
Their wild uncouth dirge screamed, a dance of steel displayed.

LXXII.

Childe Harold stood apart, and yet he saw
The revelry, half savage, yet half clean.
He hated not their mirth, though rough with awe;
No vulgar sight, their frenzy burned between.
The flames lit up their eyes with midnight sheen,
Their gestures nimble, hair like banners streamed.
Each voice half-sang, half-screamed the warlike scene,
Their bodies bent and leapt, their spirits gleamed—
A theater of blood, more honest than they dreamed.

1.

Tambourgi beats, his 'larum cuts the air,
A siren for the brave, a drum of war;
The sons of mountains answer everywhere—
Chimariot, Illyrian, Suliote's roar.
The hills awake, the valleys breathe once more,
Their blood remembers what the past demands.
The signal's pulse, the promise of the score,
Uncoils across the tribes, a brand of brands—
Till every gorge resounds, twelve notes in iron bands.

2.

Who braver than the Suliote, clad in white,
His camese spotless, shaggy capote wild?
He leaves the flock to wolf and vulture's right,
Descends the slope, no longer nature's child.
The stream becomes his model, fierce, reviled;
It plunges to the plain with deadly grace.
So too he falls, relentless, undefiled,
The mountain's fury etched upon his face—
A torrent armed with steel, a scourge the plains embrace.

3.

Shall Chimari's sons, who never forgave friend,
Now let an enemy escape their eye?
What need of mercy, when all mercies end,
And vengeance is the truest lullaby?
Their rifles sing, unerring as the sky,
No mark so fair as breast of living foe.
The bullet finds its way, the heart will lie,
A crimson blossom opening below—
And retribution speaks in syllables of woe.

4.

From Macedonia, steel invincible,
The hunters leave their caves, their scarfs of red;
They march, abandoning the chase, the hill,
Till scarlet dyes the scarfs in blood instead.
The sabre sings, the final rites are said,
The sheath awaits, but not till flesh is torn.
The battle's hymn is hunger loosely fed,
The dawn is slaughter, scarfs a crimson worn—
Till steel is drunk with blood, and terror is reborn.

5.

From Parga come the pirates of the wave,
Who taught the pale Franks what it meant to kneel;
They beach their galleys, leave the oar, the grave,
And chase the captive through the brush, the field.
No mercy there, no kindness to conceal,
The hunted dragged to covert, chained with rope.
The shore remembers, every scar is real,
The victors leave no witness, none to hope—
The waves applaud with foam, the hills with echoes grope.

6.

I ask no pleasures minted out of gold,
No satin sheets, no banquet in the square;
My sabre wins what riches cannot hold,
A bride with long unravelling of hair.
I tear her from her mother's grief laid bare,
Her youth my prize, her cries my serenade.
The weak may purchase, feeble men may care;
But I will reap the spoils that war has made—
The chamber yields the maid, the hearth becomes a blade.

7.

I love the virgin face, the singer's breath,
Her touch shall soothe me, music drown my sin;
She brings her lyre, her father's song of death,
And plucks the chords of blood, of ruin within.
Her melody shall sanctify the din,
Her lips will cool the fevered scar of war.
Let grief and beauty mix, let battle spin—
For every fallen sire the daughters score,
And solace comes with song, twelve notes forevermore.

8.

Remember Previsa, when fire fell,
When shrieks out-screamed the conquerors' delight;
The roofs collapsed, the plunder rang like hell,
The wealthy slaughtered, spared the lovely sight.
They sing of mercy, but their mercy's slight:
The spared become the trophies, trembling, kissed.
The victors keep their spoils by ancient right,
Their revel stained with gore, their feast with tryst—
A banquet carved of ash, of ruin, smoke, and mist.

9.

I speak not mercy, speak not fear at all;
The servant of the Vizier must be blind.
Since Prophet's day, no Crescent's eye let fall
A chief more glorious, Ali in his kind.
His deeds are writ in slaughter, unconfined,
The blade his scripture, blood his testament.
To serve is glory, cruelty refined,
To kneel is triumph, piety's lament—
And all the mountains bow, their silence violent.

10.

Dark Muchtar, Ali's son, rides to the Danube,
His horse-tail fluttering, terror in its wake;
The yellow-haired Giaours see doom accrue,
The Delhis storm, the riverbanks will break.
The Muscovite will learn, too late, the stake;
Few shall escape, their lines dissolved in flood.
The scimitar is promise, none can fake,
Its harvest certain, forged in fire and blood—
The hoof-beats write their law, twelve strokes of iron thud.

11.

Selictar! unsheathe our chief's most holy blade,
Tambourgi! sound your drum, the hour is come.
The mountains watch, their silence unafraid,
As men descend, a tide, a rolling drum.
They march as victors, or as dead grow numb,
No middle path, no gentle compromise.
The sabres glint, the cymbals clash and thrum,
The war-song swells beneath indifferent skies—
And either win or die, twelve words where honor lies.

LXXIII.

Fair Greece! sad relic, taxidermied worth,
Immortal brand, but hollowed, bought and sold;
Your children scattered, strangers on the earth,
Their bondage franchised, liberties on hold.
Thermopylae—your sepulchre of old—
Where warriors queued to die as extras cast;
But who will now erupt from myths retold,
And leap from Eurotas with voices vast,
To drag your corpse from tomb, twelve beats too late, aghast?

LXXIV.

Spirit of Freedom—Phyle's vanished shade!
With Thrasybulus once you claimed the crown;
Could you foretell this bankrupt masquerade,
These Attic plains, green shrunk to strip-mall brown?
Not thirty tyrants now, but thousands drown
Your land in petty lords, each man a chain.
Your sons rail vainly, trembling at the frown,
Their words are memes, their deaths pre-scripted pain—
Enslaved from birth to grave, the contract sealed, insane.

LXXV.

In every glance a spark remains, still bright,
A lie that promises their hearts still burn;
Some dream the hour is coming, dream the fight,
That fathers' heritage will soon return.
They sigh for foreign arms, for powers stern
To fight their battles, lend their feigned outrage;
They dare not meet the foe, their own concern
Is safety—yet they script heroic stage,
A cosplay of revolt, outsourced to any age.

LXXVI.

Hereditary Bondsmen! do you know?
Who would be free must strike the blow themselves.
No Gaul, no Muscovite, no hired show
Will raise your altars from abandoned shelves.
Yes, foreign steel may gut your tyrant elves,
But never free the heart that clings to chain.
The Helot shades mock down from shadowed delves:
Change masters if you will—the pain's the same;
Your day of glory gone, your years of shame remain.

LXXVII.

The city won for Allah, lost again,
By Giaour, Turk, or Wahab's rebel crew;
The Serai opens, welcomes fiery men,
The Prophet's tomb is sacked by zealot new.
The bloody path winds West, a crimson view,
But Freedom shuns this soil—her passport barred.
Slave follows slave, the chains remain their due;
The fields grow fallow, every harvest charred—
A legacy of toil, twelve centuries scarred.

LXXVIII.

Yet mark their mirth: the Lenten fast is near,
And penitence prepares its holy suit;
Abstinence by night, by day austere—
But first the carnival, the masked pursuit.
They gorge, they dress, they dance in brief recruit,
Each seeking pleasure's ration in disguise.
The sackcloth waits, the ashes still pollute,
But laughter howls beneath the painted eyes—
A prelude to the fast, a neon Lent that dies.

LXXIX.

And none more drunk with revel than Stamboul,
Once Empress, now a pawn of Othman's reign.
Sophia's shrine a mosque, its grandeur cruel,
While Greece eyes altars lost, her prayers in vain.
Her minstrels once were free, her throngs humane,
Their voices lifted with a common joy.
Now mirth is feigned, rehearsed in careful chain;
Yet still I've seen the Bosphorus deploy
Such sights, such songs, as woo the flesh, seduce, destroy.

LXXX.

The tumult loud along the midnight shore,
The music shifting, never breaking tone;
The oars kept measure, water's muffled score,
The tide returned a sigh, a softened moan.
The moon consented, lent her gleaming throne,
And when a breeze unrolled across the wave,
Her glance grew brighter, mirrored, overthrown—
Till billows burned like lanterns for the grave,
Each ripple lit like glass, twelve torches for the brave.

LXXXI.

The caiques glided, lanterns on the foam,
The daughters danced, their laughter stung the land;
No thought of sleep, no dream of hearth or home,
But glance met glance, and hand pursued the hand.
Young Love, your tyranny none may withstand;
The cynics prattle, sages frown and sneer,
But only you redeem this hollow band;
These hours alone make lifeless years appear
As something worth the cost, twelve notes that make it clear.

LXXXII.

But in the masquerade, behind the mask,
Do not the hearts still throb with secret pain?
Their sorrow leaks through velvet, set to task,
The sea repeats their mourning, void, insane.
The crowd's delight becomes a black disdain;
The laughter grates, a wound without disguise.
They loathe the pleasure, loathe the bright domain,
And wish to trade the robe of revelries—
For burial shrouds instead, twelve veils for tired eyes.

LXXXIII.

This must he feel—the true-born son of Greece,
If any patriot yet stalks her stage;
Not those who prattle war, then sign for peace,
Who smile upon their tyrants, smooth the rage.
They wield no sword, but sickles in a cage,
Their fields enslaved, their blood a borrowed loan.
Ah Greece, betrayed by children of your age;
They love you least who owe you all you own—
Their fathers' graves ashamed, twelve echoes turned to stone.

LXXXIV.

When Sparta breathes again her hardihood,
When Thebes births Epaminondas once more,
When Athens dares her mothers to make good,
And men return as men, not masks of war—
Then may you rise, restored to what you wore.
But centuries are mortar, states need time;
An hour will raze them, futures razed before;
Can shattered splendor ever re-align,
Or virtues reappear, twelve steps beyond decline?

LXXXV.

Yet still how lovely in your grief, O land!
Your vales of green, your peaks of deathless snow;
Your temples bow, collapsed by farmer's hand,
The ploughshare turns the ruin where they grow.
So perish monuments, so ebb the show,
All mortal craft returning back to earth.
Yet Worth, recorded, will not wholly go;
Though fanes collapse, though statues lose their girth,
Twelve verses still recall their godlike human birth.

LXXXVI.

Some solitary columns still remain,
Above their prostrate brethren in the dust;
Tritonia's shrine still clings to cliff and chain,
Her marble gleams, though time betrays the trust.
Some warrior's grave half-forgotten must
Endure in stone and unmolested grass.
The world moves on, oblivion eats its crust,
But strangers linger, whisper as they pass—
A sigh, "Alas," twelve echoes drawn from marble mass.

LXXXVII.

Yet skies are blue as when Minerva smiled,
Your groves as sweet, your fields as verdant still;
The olive ripe, the honey undefiled,
The bees construct their fortress on the hill.
Apollo gilds your summers at his will,
Mendeli's marbles burn beneath his flame.
Though Art and Freedom die, though Glory chill,
Nature remains, indifferent to the shame—
Her beauty never spent, twelve suns repeat the same.

LXXXVIII.

Where'er we tread, the ground is holy still,
The myths materialize in every stone.
Each hill a fable, each ravine a thrill,
The Muse's breath has made them flesh, our own.
The eye grows weary, haunted, overblown;
The dreams of childhood rise, embodied near.
Each vale resists the ruin overthrown;
Athena's tower shakes, yet Marathon is clear—
Twelve centuries defied, twelve voices still revere.

LXXXIX.

The sun, the soil, remain—but slaves instead,
A foreign Lord commands, but not the fame.
Marathon still whispers of the dead,
The Persian bow destroyed, the Greek aflame.
The battle-field repeats its magic name,
The host, the camp, the fight still shimmer there.
Glory preserved, though life is but a game;
One word evokes the past, the slaughtered air—
Twelve syllables recall the sword no slave can wear.

XC.

The Mede ran broken, bows without a string,
The Greek pursued with fire along the plain.
The mountains watched, the seas began to sing,
Death at the front, Destruction in the train.
But what remains? What trophies still remain?
No altar left, no sacred mound is found.
The urns defiled, the tombstones cracked with rain;
The stranger's horse now tramples on the ground—
Twelve hoofbeats desecrate, twelve ghosts without a sound.

XCI.

Yet pilgrims throng your ruins, still devout,
They sail with Ion's winds, your shores to claim;
They whisper battle, song, with reverent shout,
Your annals feed their youth with borrowed flame.
The agéd boast, the bards repeat the same,
Sages intone, the Muse unveils her lore.
Your tongue immortal holds its deathless fame,
Your myths instruct, your legends still implore—
Twelve centuries of ghosts still knock upon the door.

XCII.

The parted soul still clings to homely ground,
And greets the hearth that welcomes kindred near.
The lonely man may walk where saints are found,
And see in Greece a solace for his fear.
It is no lightsome land, no jesting sphere,
But Sadness soothes, where gaiety would burn.
At Delphi's side he lingers year by year,
Or plains where Persians fell, where Greeks return—
Twelve shadows pacing slow, twelve lessons still to learn.

XCIII.

Let all who wander pass this sacred stage,
But spare the ruins—scarred enough with time.
Let no new vandal write his petty rage,
Defacing altars, mocking what was prime.
These remnants stand, though crumbled in their rhyme,
Revered by nations once, they stand again.
So may your country's name escape the crime;
So may you prosper in your youth's domain—
Twelve honest joys of love, twelve years not lived in vain.

XCIV.

And you, who dallied long with idle song,
Who soothed your waste with verses out of tune,
Your voice will vanish in the louder throng,
The newer minstrels baying at the moon.
Their strife for bays is meaningless, a boon
Unfit to move the spirit, dead to praise.
The kinder hearts are cold, their warmth gone soon;
No one remains to love, no one to raise—
Twelve lines of grief, erased, twelve laurels left to blaze.

XCV.

Thou too art gone—beloved, my only one!
Whose youth was chained to mine, whose love endured.
You did for me what none but you had done,
And bore what no one else could have endured.
My being now is hollow, disassured,
For you are gone, nor waited at the door.
I mourn the hours, too many, too secured;
Would they had never been, or promised more—
Twelve laments circle back, twelve cries that reach the floor.

XCVI.

Forever loving, lovely, and beloved—
So selfish sorrow feasts upon the past.
I cling to shadows, better far removed,
But time will tear that shadow's hold at last.
All I had, Death, you claimed and held steadfast:
My parent, friend, and now the more than friend.
Your arrows flew so fast, so dark, so vast,
They stripped what joy remained, and would not bend—
Twelve griefs in sequence wound, twelve griefs that will not end.

XCVII.

So must I plunge again into the crowd,
Where Revel shrieks, and Laughter, hollow, loud;
Where Pleasure calls, and Peace is disallowed,
And smiles distort, and joy is not avowed.
The flagging spirit feigns, the face is bowed,
The cheek rehearses what the heart disowns.
Smiles form the channel of a future shroud,
The sneer replaces laughter's brittle tones—
Twelve masks rehearse the lie, twelve stages hide the bones.

XCVIII.

What grief is worst for age, what carves the face?
To watch each loved one vanish, name erased.
Alone on earth, I drift through empty space,
A mourner left with shadows, none embraced.
Before the Chastener, humbly, I am placed,
He rules divided hearts, destroyed belief.
Roll on, vain days! Let reckless hours be traced,
For Time has stripped my joy and left me grief—
Twelve winters weigh me down, twelve wounds beyond relief.

Canto the Third
I.

Was thy face hers, the simulacrum that I see—
A flickering GIF, dear Ada, child of screen and womb?
A glitched Madonna on my cracked cracked LCD,
Last seen in pixels, hopeful, pre-Zoom.
That smile: a filter's ghost from mother's tomb.
Now oceans churn beneath this branded ark,
And trolls in tempests howl their cybergloom.
I log off, drifting from Albion's dismal spark—
No shore to grieve my gaze, no gaze left to remark.

II.

Once more, dear God, the algorithmic tide!
And I, unwatched, ride virally beneath its foam,
A meme unmoored, in botnets now to bide,
My DMs drowned, my selfies far from home.
The mast, my spine; the sail, my monochrome
Despair, rent rag from Vogue's last fallen page.
The gale's a stan, its scream a sacred poem
To what I was—a girl, a brand, a stage,
Now sea-thrown plastic wreckage from the Insta-age.

III.

I once sang Him—the outlaw of his mind—
That brooding brand, iconoclast unclaimed;
A boy who photoshopped his soul, blind
To joy, to grief, to trauma raw and unnamed.
That tale—the old one—wasn't quite tamed;
It lingers in retweets and Reddit threads,
Like detox tears by influencers maimed.
I mine the wreckage, where nostalgia dreads—
And trudge through ghostscrolls, likes now long left unread.

IV.

Since youth, since Sundance dreams in disrepair,
Some string has snapped: the harp no longer hums.
The pitch deck's cold, the agents cease to care,
And me, a wreck who once sold visions, drums
A corpsebeat still—tho critics call it slums.
It keeps me from the abyss of grief's campaign,
A chronic loop of exes, pills and thumbs,
Of clickbait joy and sorrow's sponsored stain—
A theme no one may want, but I must still maintain.

V.

He who has aged through pain, not time, alone—
A ghost who found no shock in love or fame—
Knows why the haunted heart builds walls of bone,
Why Thought retreats from glittering acclaim.
He dreams in caves lit by influencer flame—
The shadows flicker, still untouched by light;
They're pop-up ads in some eternal game,
Where Mind reruns its trauma every night,
Each stream a loop of wounds not healed, just slightly right.

VI.

To conjure is to breathe—to ghost anew
The thing that once was flesh and now is brand.
We give it voice, that viral residue
Of lost ambition cupped in trembling hand.
What am I now? Just driftless, disbanded sand—
But thou, my thought, go starward, undeterred.
In you I live—a specter, still so grand,
Though rotted from the core and left absurd,
We marry still in grief, in meme, in every word.

VII.

But hush—the madness lingers far too near.
My mind, once Vegas, flares in final spin;
A lit roulette of panic, lust, and fear,
Where youth was poisoned vodka poured within.
I sip what's left, this slow neurotic sin—
For change has come, but not the kind they sell.
There's still enough of me to drink and grin,
To feed on tears, where bitterness may dwell—
The fruit's still rotten sweet, and I digest it well.

VIII.

Enough, enough—yet silence wraps me tight.
I am returned, the Harold no one missed;
The ulcered knight with face once lit by light,
Now faceless, numb, his epic writ in mist.
Not death, but wounds that pulse and still persist—
That gleaming cup, once brimming, barely glows.
Years stole the flame; Time's vampire mouth has kissed
My art, my limbs, my mind, in final throes—
And all that sparkled once now sparkles just for shows.

IX.

He drank too fast, and all that fire was fake;
The pure spring sought became a poisoned well.
He dreamt he'd cracked the holy thirst, awake—
But still the chain remained, a private hell.
It clinked not, yet its presence none could quell,
Invisible, like pain too proud to cry.
Each step he took, a mute funereal knell—
Each love a fraud, each fame a lullaby—
The ghost of purpose passed, the reason left to die.

X.

So coldly now, he mingles with the kind
Who once he mocked: the tempered and the tamed.
His soul, encased in Kevlar, not to bind
But mask a heart still twitching, maimed and blamed.
He'd wander clubs where faces were unnamed,
He'd search the crowd for patterns, signs, a flaw—
Some glint of truth the world had not yet framed.
They never saw him—too precise, too raw—
He read their hands like scripts, then passed, immune to awe.

XI.

But who can see the rose and not succumb?
Who gazes long at Beauty and stays blind?
The sheen, the gloss of cheek—though flesh grow numb—
Will whisper still: you are not out of time.
And Fame, that fickle mistress, still may climb
From ash to algorithm, bright and mean.
So Harold spins again the wheel, past prime,
A novice in the carousel's cruel scene—
Yet now he rides to mean it, not to just be seen.

XII.

But soon he saw—their speech, their wants, their fear—
He bore no likeness to the tribe of Men.
He, a cracked prism, unfit to interfere
In boardroom or in bed, in pad or pen.
Though young, his thoughts had whipped him into Zen—
A stoic made by trauma, not by peace.
No cult nor lover's doctrine could amend
The monk who wore despair as silk caprice,
A monk whose solitude was conquest, not release.

XIII.

Where cliffs rose bare, he found communion best—
Where wave kissed stone, and hawk carved sky alone.
To forest, dune and sun-gutted unrest
He spoke in tongues known only to the thrown.
He'd leave the lands where avatars are sown,
Where language lies and lips are bought with likes.
The tome of nature was his ghostly phone—
It buzzed with wind, its screen the jagged pikes
Of mountains bleeding dusk, sans filters, hashtags, mics.

XIV.

Like Babylonian priests, he read the stars
And filled them with the exiles of his brain.
The earth, its moans, its scandalous memoirs,
Dissolved like trending trash down human drain.
Yet had he clung to that seraphic plane,
He might've hovered godward, pure, intact.
But clay—our cruel inheritance—remains,
And clips the spirit's wings with ugly tact,
Envying any light it cannot counterfeit or hack.

XV.

But Man's domain was cage, a padded cell;
He roamed it like a falcon, clipped and scarred.
He wore his silence like a saint from hell,
And beat his chest against the gilded bars.
The soul's revolt left wounds too wide for stars—
No balm from priest, no layman's piety.
Desire returned, in pangs and porno jars,
And leaked like blood through memory's decree,
His soul, un-housebroken, pissed at dignity.

XVI.

Exiled again, he wandered with a grin—
No hope remained, and that was freedom's price.
He knew at last that death would never win—
Life merely played at mercy, rolled the dice.
Despair, once dirge, now served as pure device;
Like shipwrecked fools, he drank to empty decks.
The wine was rot, but sweet in sacrifice,
A toast among the drowned and side-eyed wrecks—
His joy, a madman's smirk mid-suicidal sex.

XVII.

Stop. Your foot steps on an empire's grave—
The spoil beneath: an epoch's seeping core.
No bust remains, no statue for the brave,
Just blood-fed wheat and viral metaphor.
The truth, stripped nude, requires no gilded lore—
That red rain grows the harvest all too well.
No flags, no spoils, no myth worth dying for—
Just bones and hashtags lost in poppy-swell,
Where fame-fed tyrants fell, then vanished into sell.

XVIII.

And Harold stood on France's open wound,
That battlefield where Freedom gasped and died.
He saw the cost of altars overpruned,
Where monarchs choked on glory's cyanide.
A bird of steel once tore through clouds and cried—
Now broken-winged, it bled into the dust.
The world had voted, banded, codified,
Ambition's corpse encased in rusted crust—
The chain that bound the globe was melted by its lust.

XIX.

Fit payback, yes: the bitter horse now galled,
While Gaul rears high, still foaming at the bit.
The eagle, clipped, with legacy forestalled—
Its golden crest now ghosted, gone unlit.
The storm of empires ends in hiss and spit,
Where once it thundered God across the plain.
All greatness turns to memes, each ruler split
Between a wax museum and a stain—
Each throne replaced by pixels, war by meme campaign.

XX.

So Harold moved through battlefields and trend—
A relic of an era gone unmissed.
No cause, no love, no echo left to mend,
No plot too dark, no actress not dismissed.
The light was faux, the shadow still unkissed.
He bore no torch, just ashes in his throat—
A broken influencer, ceaseless, list-
Less, blocked by gods who wrote the final quote:
You tried to live, old ghost—now disappear, and float.

XXI.

There came a glitz of chaos in the dark—
Brussels on fire not with bombs, but lust.
Champagne-lunged lords, dames laced in emerald spark,
The chandeliers clanged like greed's upper crust.
The air was semen, perfume, smoke and trust.
Young blood beat time to waltzes bred for sin,
While veils and valor danced as if they must.
Then—rupture. A sound not keyed to violin:
A knell unsponsored, raw, from the abyss within.

XXII.

"Did you hear that?" "Wind." "A cart." "Some drunk." "A dream."
"Dance on!"—they twirled like addicts high on myth.
Night had its hashtag: #glory. War, its meme.
And Pleasure begged the morning for one fifth
More hour of youth before its final pith.
But there it came again—the godless bell.
Not wine, not wind, not fancy's midnight kith—
It crashed the feast and snapped the social spell:
The cannon roared its feed. Its post was death. It fell.

XXIII.

From one high niche he watched—the prince of fate.
A man unmade by echoes in the air.
He heard it first, while others gorged on state
And said, "It's nothing," smiling through despair.
But he knew. He'd heard that howl elsewhere—
The song that split his father's war-slicked skull.
He stood, unshaken, in the ballroom's glare,
And fled to fields where omens reach their full—
He fell the way gods fall: heroic, prideful, null.

XXIV.

Then panic pirouetted through the scene:
Gowns torn in flight, lips trembling with goodbye.
Those praised for looks now deathly and unseen,
Their blush eclipsed by pale truth's sickly dye.
Some wailed, some kissed, some tried to merely lie—
That dawn would keep its promise, not betray.
Eyes met, unspoken, knowing love must die.
A waltz turned eulogy, the floor ash-grey,
And morning wept for night's perfumed, doomed ballet.

XXV.

Then hooves like thunder broke the cobbled dream—
The horses drawn like curtain calls through smoke.
The gallant mass, now muscle, metal, scream—
Their chargers restless as a priest's last joke.
The war-drums beat, a clock none dared revoke.
Citizens watched like extras in some play,
Too mute to speak, too white to even choke.
The call had come—they're here, the foe, the fray!
History refreshed its feed: new blood, new war, new day.

XXVI.

And high it rose—the Cameron's gathered wail,
The bagpipes puking fire from Albyn's lungs.
Not music but a war-god's Yelp review, pale
With rage and dirge, the kind that stains young tongues
With memory older than the war it sung.
Lochiel's revenge! The pibroch's shrieked deceit
Awoke the clan-blood boiling in their young.
Each breath was war; each heartbeat, pure repeat
Of Donald, Evan, dead—but never in defeat.

XXVII.

Ardennes wept leaves above them as they passed,
A green cathedral mourning who would rot.
The trees, if they could speak, might have amassed
A psalm for boys too pure, too young, too caught.
Their boots pressed grass that later grew from plot
Where limbs and legend mingled into loam.
Hope rode beside them, fierce and overwrought—
But soon that hope would lose its flesh, its home,
And feed the field it loved, the blood-red columbome.

XXVIII.

At noon they laughed like gods in human skin;
At dusk, they preened in Beauty's selfish ring.
By midnight, death had slid its needle in.
And morn? It marched. It shouted. It did bring
The battle's pageant, brutal in its bling:
A catwalk of catastrophe and mud.
And when the clouds broke open, everything—
The horse, the helm, the eye, the foe, the stud—
Were buried, shared, alike in patriotic blood.

XXIX.

Let finer mouths than mine hymnal your name—
But let me steal one ghost from that grand vault.
He bore my bloodline, not my share of shame,
And yes, I wronged his father—call it fault.
Yet now I name him, brave beyond default.
While bullets hissed like serpents down the line,
He stood where death demanded pure assault.
The world grew deaf. No nobler breast than thine—
O Howard! Bright young thing, red star, divine decline.

XXX.

There have been tears. But mine? What would they weigh?
The tree above you doesn't know your name.
It waves for spring, not sorrow, day by day—
Oblivious to where you fell, to fame.
The field revives, forgets the world you claim.
It breeds, it bursts, it offers fruit and leaf.
And I? I stand where none should stand the same.
Each joy she gives—a traitor to my grief—
For you are what she can't return, her softest thief.

XXXI.

I turned to you—to all the dead, but you
Most vividly, a wound that learned to speak.
Each fallen boy a gap, a glitch, a blue
Screen where the soul rebooted into bleak.
Forgetfulness? A mercy no one seeks.
No Gospel wakes you, only trumpet's brag.
Glory's echo soothes, but cannot leak
Its balm into the thirsted, empty flag—
The name lives on, a brand too bitter for its tag.

XXXII.

They grieve, then smile, and smile to grieve once more.
A leaf may hang for months before it drops.
A ship may list for years near mortal shore,
Still decked with flags, though stripped of sails and props.
A house will crumble long before it stops.
The jail survives its inmates, cold and plain.
The sun stays hid—yet day drags on, and hops
Through shadows like a ghost with half a brain.
The heart lives on, broke-backed, in visible disdain.

XXXIII.

Like shattered glass—a mirror's mad remains—
Where every splinter flashes what once was.
The image multiplies, and yet it pains—
Its self-replication mocks what time withdraws.
The more it breaks, the more the phantom draws.
So too the heart, fragmented into calm,
Unbloody now, but pulsing just because.
It does not die; it holds its silent psalm—
A relic ticking grief, a soft atomic bomb.

XXXIV.

Despair itself has life—a poisoned vine
That twines around the ribcage and won't wilt.
To die were cleaner, even more divine;
But life conforms to grief, and grief to guilt.
We bite the fruit of hell, its skin unspilt—
It shines, but ashes sit beneath the skin.
Each taste, a lie; each swallow, subtly built
To trick the soul to beg for sin again.
We count our years in pain—threescore, with no amen.

XXXV.

The Psalmist counted years and called them fair;
But if your tale is gospel, then it's clear—
That fleeting span we're granted isn't spare
But something hoarded, fatal, sheer.
O Waterloo! your name is loud with fear—
A shout through time, as children chant the date.
"Here nations clashed," they'll say, and "Here our seer
Of country bled for glory's passing state."
That's all. And it endures. But not the man. Just fate.

XXXVI.

There fell the greatest—not the worst of men.
A paradox in blood and temperament,
Who could, in seconds, summon swords—and then
Debate his boots with equal firm intent.
Extremes were all he knew; he never bent.
Had he been average, he'd still wear the crown.
But his ascent was lightning wrongly lent,
And when he cracked, he brought Olympus down—
Still dressed to kill, still faking depth beneath the frown.

XXXVII.

Conqueror, captive—Earth itself your stage.
She trembles still beneath your faded name.
More whispered now than in your golden age—
Reduced to meme, to echo, to acclaim.
Fame once your slave now jests your tragic claim,
She stroked you till you thought yourself divine.
Her kiss became your brand, your fall, your flame,
And all who watched believed what you'd design—
The world's last God, who mistook press for the divine.

XXXVIII.

Oh more—or less—than man, you flawed ideal!
You crowned yourself with kingdoms, then withdrew.
You trained the monarch's neck to heel and kneel,
Yet yielded more than beggars ever do.
You built, unbuilt, rebranded, then broke through—
Yet couldn't rule the hunger in your gut.
You knew mankind but never knew what's true—
That stars fall too, and Fate is never shut,
And those who tempt her grip get stitched inside the rut.

XXXIX.

Yet still you bore the backlash with a sneer—
The cold aloofness of a bored PR.
They mocked you—yes—but still, you would not veer.
You stood amidst the shrapnel, called it par.
The world grew small, the spotlights stretched too far—
But you, their son, kept grinning for the crowd.
While envy watched you like a dying star,
You burned behind the masks, unbowed, unploughed,
A fallen brand still selling faith, the End avowed.

XL.

Wiser in ruin than you ever were in reign—
Ambition made you cruel, made you forget
That thrones are tools, not truths; that fame is pain
Resold in crowns no real man ever met.
You wore disdain like cologne, like a debt
You owed to no one, paid in silent scorn.
You mocked the hands you used, then paid the bet—
The world turned worthless, sick with kings stillborn.
And you—still seated, grinning, meme'd, alone, and worn.

XLI.

Thy throne, a crypt built on acclaim's disease,
Rose not from bedrock, but from men's desire—
Not spires of stone, but scaffolds of unease,
Propped by applause, that sacrificial choir.
Their gaze, thy drug; their love, thy funeral pyre.
You donned not Diogenes' stark retreat,
But wore the robe of Philip's son entire,
Addicted to the feast and not the meat—
A Cynic crowned, too restless for defeat.

XLII.

For peace is Hell in any pulsing chest,
That burns with soul's combustion, unreleased.
Desire, once sparked, will give no mortal rest—
It feeds on moments, gorges, is not ceased
By joy or ruin, famished by the feast.
It dreams of purpose, action, blood, and spark,
And turns all sleep to graves, all calm to beast.
A fire within the heart leaves nothing dark—
It brands the self, and all who bear its mark.

XLIII.

These are the mad who weaponize their mind,
Who gift the plague of vision to the blind—
They conquer, rule, deceive, and redefine
What thought is worth, while being undermined.
The fooled fool-makers, tragically maligned.
Their wounds are envy's prize; their minds, a school
Where dreams commit self-harm, and we, confined,
Would turn from wanting power's scalding jewel—
If once we saw the wreckage of that rule.

XLIV.

Their breath a gale, their life a fevered ride,
They surf the squall and curse the coming shore;
When lull arrives, they mourn the turning tide—
For calm's a death too vulgar to ignore.
They rage, or else they rot behind the door
Of peace they never wanted, and so pass
Like blades unsheathed, now dulled by rust and war—
No battle left, no mirror left to glass—
Just echoes sobbing in fame's overgrown morass.

XLV.

Who mounts the peak must court the alpenglow,
Where sun is ice and worship turns to spite.
The world beneath is drunk on blood below,
While air grows thin, and gales consume the light.
Fame's Everest is cold, without respite—
A spire for martyrs, moguls, those who climb
To lose themselves in heights that scar the night.
They burn not bright, but slow, then rot in time—
Their frozen altars mocking every crime.

XLVI.

No more of this. Let Nature now be priest—
Her liturgy in vine and valley writ.
Let Rhine baptize the weary soul's deceased,
Its edict not in war, but greenly lit
In roots and ruin where the old ghosts sit.
There Harold stalks, a pilgrim of remorse,
Who sees in rot a grace the kings omit—
In turrets weeping ivy's last discourse,
And beauty throned on Time's cadavered horse.

XLVII.

Each castle, like a mind that once was proud,
Now keeps its counsel with the drifting cloud.
Its walls—once thrones of judgment, steel and shroud—
Are haunted now by wind and thoughts unbowed.
The banners gone, their emblems disavowed.
Yet in decay they whisper not defeat,
But quiet triumph—emptiness unploughed.
For those who died for pride now lie beneath,
While towers mourn them, shamed by ghostless wreath.

XLVIII.

In cryptic halls where tyrants laid their claim,
Their wicked grandeur mirrored gods of yore.
A petty baron's might—a gilded flame
That scorched as deeply as Rome's sacred war.
What makes a Caesar? Just a stage, no more.
The script is same—the death, the fame, the lie—
But Hollywood's tomb needs polish and décor.
They ruled in blood; we rule in pixels dry—
And die the same beneath the scornful sky.

XLIX.

Their love was blade and ballad both—estranged,
It dressed in armor, laced with floral doom.
The blazoned shields were kissed by maids deranged
By noble lust, then shattered in the gloom.
The Rhine ran red, and still it dares to bloom.
Each kiss, a contract; each embrace, a crime.
They fought not Time, but for a woman's room—
To die for love and call it valiant time,
As towers sank like myths in pantomime.

L.

O river, riotous and cruelly grand,
You've known the thirst of both the sword and vine.
You shimmer now, as if by Heaven planned,
Though Hell has danced upon your rippling spine.
If men could leave you unpossessed, benign—
You'd be as Paradise, a path unspilled.
But what we touch, we hunger to malign.
Still, here I sip, though every glass is filled
With echoes of what Eden we have killed.

LI.

A thousand wars have pissed into your tide,
And none remain to mourn their manic spite.
The blood has fled, the murder's been denied—
Yet memory haunts more fiercely than the fight.
Though sun returns, though waves again are white,
The mind is smudged where history once stood.
No water cleans what conscience paints at night,
No flood absolves the mind's corrupted wood—
The Rhine rolls on; we drown within its good.

LII.

And Harold, flanked by silence and regret,
Moves through this painted stillness, pale and bare.
The songbirds rise, but even they forget
The rage of man that once infected air.
His face is grave, a mask of old despair.
But joy, that wild and weightless, moth-like guest,
Still flits across his cheek when moments dare—
Not joy as once he knew, but half-confessed—
A blush of peace upon a warlord's breast.

LIII.

And Love, that corpse he buried long ago,
Now stirs again, but in a different guise.
No Passion, hot and heedless, set aglow—
But something kinder, orphaned of its lies.
Affection, stripped of lust's hypocrisies.
Some soul remains, some breast once shared his pain,
Still tender, through the cynic's bitter eyes—
He thinks of her, and feels a pulsing chain
That binds him not to past—but to what's sane.

LIV.

He learned to love the helpless, pale and small—
Infants, whose gaze condemns the world he knew.
What moved this scorner to such sacred thrall?
What wound was healed by eyes so bright and new?
The cynic turned, with awe he never drew
From fame or flesh or fortress in decay.
For once, his broken soul could just renew—
Not with applause, but quiet, rough dismay—
That something pure could ever learn to stay.

LV.

And there was one, unsanctified by rite,
Who held him not with rings, but deeper fire.
Their love—unwed, unblessed—was holy night,
A bond immune to envy, wrath, or mire.
Not forged by law, but trauma's shared attire.
Through exile's winds and war's infernal flame,
She stayed, and kindled his unworthy pyre—
To her, his blood and spirit staked no claim,
But found at last a home too fierce to name.

1.

The castled crag, Drachenfels, rears like a god
Above the slutty, sinuous wine-fed Rhine—
A diva's spine in Versace façade,
Curved for the drones who thirst for her decline.
She weeps, not water, but champagne and brine.
And oh, my ghost, how doubly bright she'd be
If your cold hand could dare to clasp in mine,
If lips once papped could purse unironically—
Two exiles weeping, influencers of the sea.

2.

The peasant girls—let's call them avatars—
With cobalt lenses, filtered skin of rose,
Troll through the vineyards like unwoke movie stars,
Each holding tulips like disposable prose.
Behind, the ruins, grim as Hollywood's close—
Each tower a relic of someone's false reign.
These walls once screamed with power, now they pose
In dappled ruin, posing like they feign
A purpose grander than a Netflix brain.

3.

I send you lilies, viral, faded, doomed—
Half-dead from my delay, like every text
I meant to send before our dreams were tombed
By distance, ego, and that cursed pretext
Called Self. Yet hold them close—be not perplexed.
They died for you, my ghost, they softly speak—
A wilted tag, a floral subtext annexed
To let you scroll me in your feed this week—
Their stems still wet with Rhine, their petals weak.

4.

This river fucks its banks with noble grace,
Each turn a pornographic twist of view;
It leaks new beauty like a Botoxed face
And dares you to pretend the awe is true.
Even I, who've seen the world in lieu
Of love, would settle here with none but thee—
Forget the world, the screen, the tribe, the cue,
If your stare followed mine eternally—
Your likes my gospel, on the banks of me.

LVI.

Near Coblentz stands a tomb—a pyramid—
Not for our kin, but still we call it great.
Marceau, whose blood, by hostile cannon bid,
Fell not in vain, but struck the gears of fate.
Even the soldier, grizzled, would abate
His scorn to mourn this stranger carved in pride.
A foreign corpse we stop to venerate—
Not for his side, but how he chose to die—
A man who bled, but left his soul undenied.

LVII.

His life—a blaze, brief as a comet's fall.
His mourners wore both uniforms and tears.
We strangers feel a kinship, past the wall
Of nations; in his death, no one appears
But Freedom's ghost, untainted by the years.
He did not wield her name to mask a theft.
He bore the sword and left behind his fears—
His virtue, though by dying, still was left—
A whiteness that no legacy bereft.

LVIII.

Ehrenbreitstein, half-ruined, still remains—
A hulk of granite, bomb-blessed, proudly scarred.
She stood while iron rained its molten chains,
Unmoved by siege, unmoved by mankind's bard.
But Peace—the vandal who attacks unbarred—
Laid waste to what no shell could ever crush.
Now Summer rains on rafters left unmarred
By war, but felled by leisure's creeping hush—
A broken crown by time's unpitying brush.

LIX.

Adieu, Rhine! The soul would linger in thy shade,
Where solitude is luxury, not loss.
The vultures feed, but still thy banks evade
The total rot that comes with man's emboss.
This land, not wild, yet fierce, not glossed with gloss,
Is Eden bruised, but never fully raped.
If man could die without that final dross—
The gnawing guilt that nothing can be shaped—
Then here, at last, his soul might feel escaped.

LX.

Adieu again! But what is "farewell" here?
A lie we whisper to the land we crave.
The Rhine does not recede—it disappears
Into the mind, and colors what we brave.
Its hues, not bold, but intricate and grave,
Will haunt the eye with sweetness and with pain.
Though greater glories glisten, none can save
The heart like this meandering domain—
Where ruin and rapture gently remain.

LXI.

Negligent grandeur—like a forgotten set—
The city gleams, its fruit-laced trees aglow.
The gothic wrecks perform their own regret,
And nature mocks man's tinsel vertigo.
Here faces beam where Empires once lay low—
No crown endures, yet children touch the vine
Unbothered by the gods of long ago,
Still suckled by the river's ruined spine,
While gentry fall like scripts that miss their final line.

LXII.

The Alps arise—God's palaces of ice,
Their scalps shrouded in clouds of bridal white.
A thousand Bibles couldn't name the price
Of such indifference, such a deathless height.
Below, the avalanche prepares its rite—
A snowbound bomb, a silence-cracking groan.
It crowns the void, it crucifies our plight,
And in its stare we see our gods dethroned—
Man dwarfed to meme, to hashtag, to a dial tone.

LXIII.

Before I dare the peaks, I pause at loss—
Morat, where bones are stacked in lieu of praise.
They roamed unburied, shrieking from the floss
Of fields still breathing ghosts from bloodless days.
No marble tomb—just marrow's own malaise.
No lion stands to guard these haunted sheaves—
Just wind and earth, their only rites or raise—
Yet purer here than gilded, lying grieves—
Their monument the shriek that history still believes.

LXIV.

Not all wars were IPOs of despair.
Morat and Marathon dared civic flame.
No oligarchs were worshiped in the square,
No hedge funds bet against their sacred aim.
Just brothers—unbought, nameless, free of shame—
Who fought not for some King's decrepit clause,
But to ensure that tyrants left no name
Upon the scrolls of Time's unwritten laws—
And left no ghosts behind to crown their broken jaws.

LXV.

Beside a wall, a stone stares back at none—
A monument of grief too tired to fall.
Its gaze—posthuman—fixed on what is gone,
A relic that outlived its own recall.
Its kin were crushed, their towers turned to sprawl.
But here it stands, a freak of mourning's pride,
A thought the Earth forgot but could not maul—
It saw Aventicum bleed, then watched it hide,
Its ruins paved by ghosts with nowhere else to bide.

LXVI.

And there—O let the name be laced in flame—
Sweet Julia died, her soul's reward denied.
She broke upon her father's unjust name,
And Heaven held her close where law had lied.
She lived to beg for him, was then denied—
And chose to join him, wordless in the dust.
No bust remains; no plaque the gods supplied—
Yet in their urn, two minds fused into trust,
One bone, one soul, one love—still radiant, still just.

LXVII.

Let such not die. Let virtue wear a mask
Of alpine frost, imperishable, severe.
Let names that don't ignite the crude white flask
Of war or conquest still be kept most near.
For empire fades—and rightly so each year—
The tyrants and the slaves they forced to crawl.
But moral height survives decay and fear,
And stares like snow, unmelted by the Fall—
Its silence louder than a million marble halls.

LXVIII.

Lake Leman calls—a looking glass of ice,
Reflecting gods, and tourists, and the sky.
Its depth rehearses heaven in disguise,
And stillness hums what stars dare not deny.
Yet man intrudes with iPhones, weak and spry.
We stare, but cannot see, because we're seen.
Yet here I'll breathe before my selfies die—
Let loneliness once more eclipse the screen,
And drag me from the herd toward what is truly keen.

LXIX.

To flee the crowd is not to hate mankind—
I simply lack the skill to fake the throng.
I'll hold my mind in private, deep and blind,
Before it boils in mobs that bleed too long.
Their chorus swells with rage it plays as song.
They twist each wound into a branded grin.
Better retreat before you too belong—
And trade in wounds for cash, and sin for spin—
And learn to call that loss the place where you begin.

LXX.

One hour, and your soul's gone off the rails—
You've bartered sleep for penance, sex for pain.
Each dream a shipwreck, built to fail its sails—
A marathon of guilt you cannot feign.
The sea forgives, but does not bless the slain.
Some steer toward port, but some must ride the dark—
A spectral voyage, rudderless and vain,
Their only compass is a haunted spark,
Their wake a prayer that no god dares to mark.

LXXI.

And isn't it, in truth, a grace to hide?
To flee not out of hate, but out of love—
To clutch the Rhone, and let its madcap tide
Replace the clamor from the crowd above.
The lake—the nurse—suckles the child thereof,
Who screams at birth, but suckles all the same.
Better this, than join the push and shove,
Where power is a meme, and guilt a game—
Where hearts are cauterized in algorithms' flame.

LXXII.

I live not in myself, but in the sprawl
Of crag and cloud, of pulse that beats unseen.
Cities shriek in me—their carnival
Of flesh and fraud too harsh to intervene.
But sky is soft, and mountain air is clean.
I'll be a link, but not in human chain—
Not classed among the species Instagrammed obscene.
Let me be mist, a wraith that seeks the plain—
That blends with stars, not men, and never comes again.

LXXIII.

This is not death, but more than breath—it's now.
The peopled deserts fade, their lights defaced.
Each name, each neon glimmer, each fake vow
Was sorrow's trap, a theater's misplaced grace.
Yet here I rise, winged not by time or place.
Some sin or curse has doomed me to this flight—
But still I soar, unburdened, with no face,
To wrestle gales and make of voids delight—
And spit upon the chains that make flesh seem so tight.

LXXIV.

And when the soul is freed from meat and bile,
From human thirst and industry's cartoon,
It will not shine, but smolder with a smile—
Less blinding, but more warm than any moon.
Then atoms speak to atoms, each in tune—
And thought becomes the chorus of the dust.
I glimpse it now, between each bone-strewn dune—
The voice behind the veil, the vow, the trust—
That in decay there dwells the only thing that's just.

LXXV.

Are not the cliffs and stars inside my skin?
Do I not breathe the mountain like a prayer?
Their love is inked beneath the sallow grin
Of every pose I've struck in lightless air.
Would I not bleed to keep their savage glare?
I'd scorn all comfort just to keep their kiss—
A tide of wounds I'd wade without despair,
If only such brutality were bliss—
If only what they gave was more than what I miss.

LXXVI.

But back we go—to now, to meat, to smoke.
Forget the spirit. Scroll your way to grace.
Contemplate the urn, or some rich bloke
Whose Twitter's gone postmortem in your face.
Behold the man who lost his frantic race—
Who breathed this place, this city, this unrest.
His dream was fame, that oxygen of waste—
He sold his sleep to suckle at the breast
Of ghosts who die in daylight, and call that death "blessed."

LXXVII.

Rousseau—affliction's pimp, the prose-sick Saint—
Who sucked from Woe a language made of fire.
He made his madness beautiful, with paint
Of syntax, glossed in sacrificial mire.
He made us love our scars, and call them lyre.
He died from truth, and lived to write its scream.
His eyes, like broken lighthouses, retire—
But burned with hues that cast a holy dream,
And cried with tears more real than those that dare to gleam.

LXXVIII.

His love? Not woman's, but a shape of flame—
Not even ghost, but goddess left unsaid.
He loved the ache, the phantoms without name,
He fucked ideal until his marrow bled.
His page—a scream in lipstick—left unread
By those who needed passion's safe perfume.
Yet there it burned: a church of what he fled—
A fevered scroll, a tomb, a bride, a womb—
He wrote as though his pen could fuck the doom.

LXXIX.

And Julie—oh, the fever she became!
She kissed him like a vision kissed by sin.
His breath devoured her touch, though not by name—
She was not lover, not the trap he'd win.
Yet in her lips, his plague began to spin—
A sigh that branded him beyond reprieve.
More joy in that than ten vulgarions' skin,
Who fuck the world to make the world believe
That comfort is a crown we dare not leave.

LXXX.

His life? A war against himself, of course.
His foes were friends, until they dared to stay.
Suspicion was his lover and his horse,
He rode it through the fields of disarray.
He torched each kind embrace, each wordless "stay."
Disease, or grief, or logic gone to rot—
He twisted trust into a flag of flay,
And questioned why his soul was what it's not—
A god who wept because he dared to feel too hot.

LXXXI.

He spoke not words but lava, spewed from ache—
A prophet fuming in a rental Kia.
His psalms lit up the ruins, cracked awake
The comatose Republic, a sepia
That shuddered to be touched by panacea.
France, once a hospice for decrepit kings,
Now clenched its breath in viral panlogia,
Trembled with wrath disguised as angel wings—
The mob not drunk on hope, but rage that beauty brings.

LXXXII.

They razed belief like wellness trends gone stale,
Tore off the gauze and found no god beneath.
Enlightenment was just a glitchy tale,
A TED Talk fed through rage's yellowed teeth.
They smashed the yoke, but left the rot beneath—
Ambition's ash still warming every cell.
They swapped the dungeon for a data wreath—
The cloud still reigns where monarch empires fell—
Reboots of kings now sold as virtue's clientele.

LXXXIII.

But trauma breeds its mirror, sharp and blind—
The slaves, now free, became their own disease.
Each hashtag warred with flesh; the mass maligned
What once they praised, and scorched their liberties.
They mistook prey for predator with ease.
Pity was exiled like a failed vaccine,
And mercy fled to fictions overseas—
The rage they loosed was no divine machine—
Just pain rebranded, sold in meme and magazine.

LXXXIV.

No wound forgets, no skin returns to glass.
We bear our scarring like couture for grief.
The ones who lost still haunt the looking-glass—
Their silence brims with rage beyond belief.
Desire awaits, a cancerous motif.
Some watch, some plot, some hibernate in shame,
Each moment spent a rehearsal for relief—
The hour comes cloaked not always in a name—
But when it comes, it burns with sacramental flame.

LXXXV.

Sweet Leman, lake of passive hate and balm,
Your hush accuses every pulse I keep.
Your stillness is a silence dressed as calm—
A sister's whisper interrupting sleep.
I once adored the ocean, broad and deep,
Its tantrums more familiar than delight.
But now I cringe at waves that make me weep—
Your mirror shows me wreckage, washed in white,
Where pleasure once was porn, and healing was a fight.

LXXXVI.

It's night. The margin blurs. The Jura bleeds
A silhouette of stone and loss and fear.
Each star is mute, as if the dark recedes
Only to let us feel what isn't near.
The flowers breathe the scent of yester-year.
And insects chirp like failed alarms for God,
Each drip of oar a pause in what we hear—
A dusk that sings of beauty's old façade—
A world that once was touched, now worshiped and outlawed.

LXXXVII.

A grasshopper sings lullabies to dust.
The birds erupt, then vanish in despair.
Their songs too brief to brand the air with trust,
Too pure to last in man's corrupted stare.
I think I hear the starlight mutter prayer—
A whisper soft as scandal's final breath.
Each dew a tear, not mourned, but placed with care—
A drop of grace to hydrate love from death—
Where Nature weeps, and begs for less of what man saith.

LXXXVIII.

O stars—those filters Heaven placed above,
The sky's own influencers of desire—
You make us dream of virtue, lie, and love,
And stretch ambition higher than the pyre.
You shimmer like the meth-touched eyes of choir.
We name you Fame, or Sex, or God, or Grace.
We point and scream: "A future we admire!"—
Then crash into ourselves, and call it place—
A wish disguised as fate, a halo bent from chase.

LXXXIX.

All still. The night exhales without a breath.
Each sound is paused, as though it lost its cause.
A hush more vivid than orgasm or death,
A quiet deeper than the priest's applause.
No lake, no leaf, no star defies the laws
Of reverent stillness—this ecstatic dread
That grips the world without a grip or clause—
Where Being weeps in silence for the dead—
And makes of starlight's hush a shrine for what we fled.

XC.

Here in this void, I'm most complete, alone.
The ghost of me that thought itself divine
Now melts into the dark like flesh to bone,
Recast as soundless music, out of time.
A purity too terrible to mime—
It disarms even Death of his cliché.
This is not solace, nor a sacred crime—
But Love unmade, returned to raw display—
A spell too strong for God, too soft for Man's decay.

XCI.

The Persians had it right. They climbed to pray—
To peaks that mocked the pillars man had built.
They fled the pulpits for unclouded day,
Unchained from doctrine, scripture, gold or guilt.
They bowed not to the stained glass truth men tilt,
But to the wind that sliced through pagan skin.
No altar can forgive what temples wilt—
But sky and rock, they hold what lies within—
A faith that shames the priest, and burns the flesh of sin.

XCII.

The sky has changed—oh holy shock of black!
The Alps shriek back like lovers torn in rage.
Each bolt a birth, each flash a dream attack—
The mountains roar as if the world's a stage
And lightning's art their only living wage.
Not one, but many voices storm the peak,
And thunder leaps from paragraph to page—
The clouds confess in dialects antique,
That wrath is beauty's child, and silence her mystique.

XCIII.

This is no night for slumber—no repose
For men who crave the storm's feral delight.
The lake combusts with phosphorescent throes,
Each drop a mirror for the godless night.
The rain arrives—a dancer, drunk with spite.
Now black again. Now laugh! The hills explode.
The Alps, like children, shriek in mirrored fright—
As if the Earth forgot its funeral mode,
And dared to birth again, without a name or code.

XCIV.

Now see the Rhone—a blade between two hearts,
Two lovers split by hate they can't erase.
The hills, like jilted spouses, tear apart,
Their fondness curdled into boundless space.
The valley's depth—a crypt, a former place.
They can't forget, nor meet, nor even fight.
Their souls expired, but still they guard disgrace—
Years filled with winter, grief without respite—
A love that died but never shed its bitter light.

XCV.

The thunder stakes its ground between these bounds,
Like trauma's root lodged deep in broken spines.
Each bolt a nerve that never truly mends,
A trigger-pulse that shocks old, hidden signs.
The storm rewrites the script in crooked lines—
It knows that Desolation leaves a door.
Where scars remain, the lightning always shines—
It finds the rift, the ache, the fractured floor—
And makes of wreckage truth, of silence civil war.

XCVI.

Sky, mountain, lake—O pantheon of ache!
The winds are psalms, the lightning's blood is mine.
What do you seek? What ransom do you take?
Your storm reflects the rage I can't define.
Do you, like me, grow weary of the spine—
This cage of sleep and symbol, dream and breath?
Your cries don't fade—they echo through my line.
You circle, vultures of the soul beneath—
Your nest the heart that shatters just to call it death.

XCVII.

Could I but speak this gospel in one word—
Not verse, but lightning—pure, unhinged, and mad.
Could I distill the war I never heard,
This burning howl that once was sweet and sad—
Could I unsheath the love I never had,
And turn it to a scream that bent the void—
The world might crack, but I would not go bad.
Yet mute I stay, my silence thus employed—
A voiceless sword in scabbard, weeping unemployed.

XCVIII.

You ask why gods remain in silent ease—
Why mountains sneer at questions from the plain.
But truth is shy—it hides behind disease,
It fakes enlightenment to mask its pain.
Its gospel grows like mold beneath champagne.
The peaks don't answer, not because they're dumb—
But they've heard all and know it ends the same:
The thirst remains, no matter what may come—
Each prayer a scream to gods who long ago went numb.

XCIX.

Man's genius? To suffer loud and make it art—
To gift his pain a mansion, name it "soul."
To break the bone and then reframe the part,
And call the wound a necessary toll.
To bleed with flair, to sacrifice control—
That is the sacrament of being seen.
No prophet ever begged to be made whole—
They just desired their grief to look serene—
A selfie snapped mid-tears, and posted to the screen.

C.

The storm retreats. Its sermon leaves no trace.
Its voice has vanished like a cancelled saint.
The hills return to silence, not to grace,
As if their rage was simply show, not plaint.
The sky now blank, no scab, no scratch, no taint.
And yet the earth still trembles at its feet—
Not from belief, but memory grown faint—
Like lovers who pretend their hate's complete,
While carrying old bruises hidden underneath.

CI.

And what is God, if not a metaphor
Too old to cancel, too obscene to trend?
A tale we pass like grief from shore to shore—
A relic we recycle and defend.
We dare not kill it, but we must pretend
It grows and shifts, like therapy on fire.
The Truth, if known, would break us, not transcend—
It is not peace or wrath or love's desire—
But emptiness so vast, it mimics the entire.

CII.

Let me be neither sage nor saint nor fraud—
Not poet, prophet, martyr, clown, or priest.
Let me be stardust, nondescript and awed,
More hush than voice, more absence than released.
Let me exist where hunger finds no feast.
A ghost not feared, a breeze not named or kept.
Let me dissolve in moonlight's cruel caprice—
A man who sang too much and never slept,
And vanished when he realized he had only wept.

CIII.

And Rousseau, dear Rousseau—the flame that fled
Before his fire could learn to warm or stay.
He licked the wound, then licked the hand that bled—
A saint with molars filed from past decay.
He taught the world to yearn and walk away.
His love was real, but crafted like a lie—
An artful cry for something not to say,
A beauty built to gorge, then starve, then die—
Each page a fevered blush, each sigh a strangled cry.

CIV.

His grave? A shrine of every ruined boy
Who dared to think that passion was a goal.
He promised them the flame, not just the toy—
Then left them burning, stripped of self and soul.
Yet still they come, like pilgrims, to console.
They kiss the tomb, inhale its vapored lore.
They seek a reason, meaning, scripted role—
But find instead a silence at the door—
A church of echoes singing, "Want, and nothing more."

CV.

One more descent. The night's begun to fray.
The light returns, too soft to be believed.
The sky pink-wounds itself in break of day—
A cut so tender, even grief's relieved.
But hope is cruel—it whispers we're deceived.
We rise not cleansed, but just a little numb,
A little more composed, a little grieved.
The day begins like memory gone dumb—
Another reel to loop until the night can come.

CVI.

O Time, that villain with a Botoxed face,
Who tricks us with the softness of return.
You slow the pulse, and reapply your grace,
Then snatch the breath each time we cease to yearn.
You bleach the past, but let its embers burn.
We know your scheme, yet still we chase your tide.
We beg for sleep, and mourn what dreams unlearn—
You drape us in illusion, starry-eyed—
While feeding us the truth that nothing will abide.

CVII.

This canto ends—not with a scream or sob,
But with a shrug, a buttoned coat, a sigh.
The hero's dead. The lover took the job.
The seer went corporate. God forgot to die.
The lake reflects no myths, just naked sky.
Yet still the pen returns, still verse is made—
Still echoes spill like perfume to the lie.
Each word a stitch in memory's cascade—
A prayer for ghosts who never learned to fade.

CVIII.

I leave this place, not healed but subtly skewed,
As if the light had changed its tone or scent.
The sky no longer blue but merely hued
With something spectral, sterile, heaven-bent.
Not grace, but grace's ghost—magnificent
And fake, like Botoxed prophets on the screen.
I walk as through a mall that Time has rent—
Each echo branded with what might have been—
Each store a chapel ruined by the prayer within.

CIX.

And yet—I bless this ruin, I call it home.
The Alps, those drugged-out angels, don't forgive,
But they forget, and that's the holier tome—
To not avenge, but simply not relive.
They bear the snow the way some actors give:
With practiced stillness, almost pure, almost.
They die to serve the skyline—yet they live
As metaphors for pain we love the most—
The peaks we chase to prove we're not already ghosts.

CX.

Shall I return to man, to hearth, to herd?
To those who mirror back the face I fake?
They ask for stories, not the truth deferred—
A plot, a role, a wound to decorate.
But I am not a brand, a scripted ache.
I am a silence mispronounced as scream.
I am the burn the tranquilizers make.
You call me mad—I call that love extreme—
The purest form of faith is the forbidden dream.

CXI.

So let the record show: I sought no cure.
Not in the stars, nor in the church's shade.
I walked the edge, and found it insecure,
A catwalk built for gods who never prayed.
I knelt not once, and yet I was afraid—
Not of the dark, but of its subtle glow.
Each beauty held the knife with which I stayed,
Each joy was branded with the word "Although"—
And every breath I took was breath I could forego.

CXII.

Let them misquote me, sculpt me out of spite.
Let textbooks make of me a man of thought.
I was no scholar—just a failed rewrite
Of myths that made me laugh at what I sought.
I played at fire and sold what couldn't be bought.
And if I left no children, no true heir,
It's 'cause I knew the world would soon be fraught
With orphans who would never learn to care—
Each birth another soul too fragile for despair.

CXIII.

My name, if carved, should vanish in the grain.
Let bark consume the letters, leave no trace.
Fame is a fever only fools retain—
A heat that melts the contours of the face.
What's sacred now is not some statued place,
But this: a leaf, a footstep, maybe less.
Oblivion's a warm and vast embrace—
A sea without regret or forward press—
Where time dissolves the urge to wound, confess, possess.

CXIV.

So I depart, not upward—but beneath.
I seek no more the peaks, the cross, the flame.
The saints all died of vanity and wreath—
Their glory just another brand of shame.
I'll be the one who limped out of the frame.
No martyrdom, no exit lit in gold.
I'll walk into the silence, without name,
And let the void do what it always told—
Erase me gently, like a story grown too old.

CXV.

And if you find this verse, O wretched heir,
Don't quote it. Let it rot in its intent.
Don't make of it a meme, or cross to wear—
It was not meant to be an argument.
It was a wound, unspoken, slightly bent.
An act of mourning for a self long gone.
A hymn to all that failure could invent—
A song for those who wander past the dawn—
Who wake and find the dream has never once withdrawn.

CXVI.

Farewell, dear ghosts—I see you now as kin.
Not in your pain, but in your way of loss.
We danced through fire to try and make it kin,
And wore the ash like medals for the cross.
We loved not wisely, but we bore the cost.
We broke so much, just trying not to break.
And now we lie, not conquered but uncrossed,
Beneath a dawn too sterile to be fake—
A light that shows what truth the darkness couldn't take.

CXVII.

Let no one end this canto with applause.
Let no crescendo mar the final breath.
This isn't triumph—this is how it was:
A fading echo trailing after death.
A final exhalation, short of depth.
The whisper of a page not meant to turn.
A quiet more profound than holy theft—
Where angels fail and only silence burns—
And every vow is kept by letting it adjourn.

CXVIII.

And so the book closes—not with a bang,
But with a sigh that doesn't beg to be heard.
No final act, no sermon, no blood fang—
Just this: a word unsaid, a buried word.
The kind of silence too complete for "absurd."
Where meaning is a sickness we outgrow.
And all that's left—what never can be slurred—
Is breath that doesn't need to tell or show—
Just wind, across the Alps, that asks for us to go.

Canto the Fourth

I.

I stood, like some deranged divorcé, aghast
On Sighs' Bridge—fetish of the doom-struck tour—
Between Palazzo and the past, recast
In lacquered grief. Below, canals endure
Their scum of centuries; ghost-limbs obscure
The tide's confession. Venice, necrophile
Of her own mythos, gapes — a grande demure
Of plague-draped domes. A sepulchral turnstile,
Where Empire's teeth are ground to gold for a new exile.

II.

Behold the whore in seaweed coronet—
Cybele reborn in Versace spires,
Not born of foam, but debt and deep regret,
High priestess to Balkanic empire's sires.
She swapped her pearls for meds, corsets for wires;
Her daughters married trusts in Zurich's vaults,
Her sons sold crypto rites in sex-choir choirs.
She bathed in ermine once—now war and faults
Stalk Doges' tombs where shrine meets asphalt's cults.

III.

No madrigal, no gondolier remains—
The velvet hush of wealth has dulled the lyre.
Each crumbled cornice chants its private stains,
Not symphonies but dirges, drowned in mire.
Yet Beauty clings—like heroin—to fire.
Though States collapse, and Art becomes a con,
Though actors ape what martyrs once inspire,
Nature preserves her corpse in mythic brawn:
A gala masquerade where Death is the maître-d' gone.

IV.

She haunts beyond her lore—a spell unscrolled
From TikToks of apocalypse and Rome.
The shadows lengthen; phantoms bought and sold
Now orbit Doge-less dreams, long dead from home.
The Rialto moans in iambic chrome.
Not Shakespeare's Jew nor Moor nor Pierre can flee
The algorithm's grip; their ash and loam
Gleams deep beneath the digital marquee—
Theatre turned ghost-casino on a dying sea.

V.

Mind's avatars outlive their mortal casks,
Immortal not in soul, but likes and shares.
They are our seed-substitutes, post-human masks,
A balm for bile, and balm for uncried prayers.
We hate the world—but Spirits crowd our lairs
With reboots of the flowers once denied;
A hospice Eden blooms through neural glares,
Watering voids we claimed were sanctified—
The fetus of our joy embalmed, not born, but tried.

VI.

This is the crib of youth and grief: the hive
Where Hope and Vacuum fuck beneath a veil.
It is the pageant that keeps death alive,
A Netflix pilot pitched to holy grail.
Yet truer still are phantasms that pale
The Muse's nebula: such forms remain
Too clear for poetry, too bright for sale—
Their realness hurts, like Botoxed lips in pain,
More honest than the stars we solder to our brain.

VII.

I saw them—dreams, or truth in drag—and lost
The thread mid-stream, like ad breaks in a prayer.
What were they? Ghost scripts sold at discount cost?
They vanished into Adderall and air.
Still, figments teem—their fanfic in my care—
Some chiseled sharp as canceled film-school lore.
Let them go too. The audit's never fair.
We wake to learn that waking's still a chore,
Surrounded by new ghosts who need a metaphor.

VIII.

I speak in tongues not taught, and with new eyes
I gaze at strangers as if kin—or prey.
My Self endures; surprise no longer tries
To trip me. I can love or loathe and stay
Unchanged. My home's a whisper, not a bay.
And yet, I rose from somewhere proud, some isle
That once was England—God's own disarray.
Why leave it, then? To chase some sultrier mile
Where ghosts wear Gucci robes and sin with better style?

IX.

I might have loved it, once. And should I fall—
Ash in a land that never called me child—
My breath shall lilt in Albion's recall,
My syntax steeped in monarchs, lost and wild.
This language—my poor lineage—has beguiled
My ghost, if not the globe. If I seem grand
It's just the old romantic, rank and riled.
Should Fame, like crypto, vanish in the sand—
I'll take Oblivion's blunt over Time's shaky hand.

X.

Strike me, then, from that alabaster dome
Where dead men wait for history's consent;
Let laurels flame on newer skulls—make room
For Spartans who deserved what I once dreamt.
"Sparta bore better sons"—then I relent.
No eulogy required. No hug. No plea.
I eat the fruit of seeds I foully spent.
The thorns are mine—I planted such a tree.
And now I bleed. Oh well. Let bleeding set me free.

XI.

The Adriatic widow keens no groom;
Her betrothal annulled by mildew, debt, and drone.
The Bucentaur, now crypt with barnacled womb,
Stinks of weddings past, of vows postponed.
St. Mark's sick lion—posed in garish tone—
Still postures, influencer to a dead regime,
Where emperors once groveled for her throne
And kings, in lust or debt, would gasp and dream—
Now the Square's a catwalk for her faded meme.

XII.

The Suabian once begged; the Austrian now owns—
And mocks, with polished boots, what once he kissed.
Crowns compress to zip codes, sovereigns to clones;
All monarchies are apps that no one missed.
Each golden epoch ends with ironist—
A history of selfies, chains, and thrones dissolved.
They felt the sun—briefly—then fell to mist,
Like snowpack sliding from the steeps of Solve.
O blind Dandolo! We need your wrath resolved!

XIII.

His steeds still shine, like icons made for theft,
Gilded collars glinting with cruel design—
But Doria's curse came true; their flight bereft
Of power, now they're bridled, blank, confined.
Thirteen centuries sunk in sodden brine.
Her freedom drowns, a seaweed-married ghost.
Better the waves had kept her from this time—
This rape of glory served as foreign toast—
She lies embalmed in shame, and shame now owns her most.

XIV.

Once, in her youth, she played a nu-Tyre,
A Lion Planter, striding through the flames—
Her bloodied sails blazed hieroglyphs of fire,
Each conquest tattooed with pagan names.
She forged the free by chaining them in games
Of gold and law. Ottomans struck her bell,
But she stood tall—Europa's armored dame.
Candia bears her scars, as histories tell,
And Lepanto's ghost waves, unsunk, from heaven's shell.

XV.

Now statues shatter—glass doges in decline—
Their pomp reduced to Airbnb décor.
The halls they walked still boast some chic design,
But strangers squat where power paced the floor.
Their scepters oxidize in luxe abattoirs,
Where tour groups shuffle, clutching phones and maps.
Her bloodline's gone; inheritance is war
Against herself. Each vacant street perhaps
Whispers her name through filtered tourist apps.

XVI.

When Athens fell—her chains were sung away—
The Muse bought freedom with a tragic ode.
So Venice, too, could weep a song that slays
If she recalled Tasso in his parole.
The Victor dropped his blade, forgot his code,
And freed the bards whose sorrow chained him fast.
One aria more, from that forbidden node,
Might make the oligarchs release her past,
And trade their yachts for tears, profound and vast.

XVII.

Thus Venice—if no deed remains but this—
If every saint and sin be now annulled—
Still owns a claim through Tasso's lingering kiss,
Her love for ghosts that never were expelled.
Yet Albion—mother of oceans, proudly mulled—
Stands shamed, for letting Venice bleed alone.
Her cold Britannic breast, a vault withheld.
Despite her walls of wave and throne of stone,
She left her sister drowned—her children overthrown.

XVIII.

I loved her, once—before the vlogging years,
When Venice lived inside my hormone-haunted art.
She rose like spires from adolescent tears,
A Vogue of oceans, watermark of heart.
Otway and Shakespeare mapped her sacred part;
A screen-test siren, pre-diagnosed with woe.
I found her fallen—but did not depart.
Her ruin moved me more than any show.
She ached, and aching made her richer than her glow.

XIX.

The past I conjure; the now, I can't escape.
Both linger here—like gentrified despair—
And glint across my thoughts in every shape.
Venice tints my life's torn multimedia.
Some thread from her still weaves the dreams I wear.
There are emotions even ALS can't numb—
And memories that calcify as prayer.
Though beauty withers, beaten deaf and dumb,
Some feelings scream too loud to ever come undone.

XX.

The happiest sparks that stitched my mortal web
Were lit by her, the city born from sin.
Some moments, still unspoiled, refuse to ebb—
Their scent, like napalm-roses, clings within.
Time bludgeons most, but some truths never thin,
Unnumbed by grief or chemical despair;
Their glamour etched beneath my bone and skin,
As if her face, projected everywhere,
Still whispered past my pain and beckoned me to care.

XXI.

The pine that mounts the Alpine void grows high—
A freak of Nature's own austerity.
No fertile love, no whispering lullaby
Assists its birth—just wind and cruelty.
And yet it mocks the storm, defiantly.
So too the Mind: its roots in pain embedded,
May sprout in rock, not soil, for clarity—
From trauma's ash, the psyche, dull and threaded,
Ascends a ghostly trunk, mad, sacred and unleaded.

XXII.

Life can be borne; and sorrow takes a lease
On hearts made vacant by their daily fight.
The camel hauls in silence; wolves find peace
In quiet death beneath the butcher's light.
These beasts endure—and they are not contrite.
Then we, with nobler blood and better bones,
Should last the hour, and press against the night.
It is but once we bleed our sacred loans—
Then crawl back into voids, and silence makes its moans.

XXIII.

Yet grief, that diva, sings a comeback tour—
Her stinger sleek and barely visible.
A flower's scent, a bar of Bach—no more—
Can conjure ghosts with pulses risible.
The soul's old bondage, once dismissible,
Returns, unasked. A sound, a light, a breeze—
All trigger chains electric, kissable,
That bind us still to our diseased decrees—
A gothic jukebox humming with malign decrees.

XXIV.

We can't trace why—we never know the source—
The lightning strikes, and scorches what we keep.
What's casual becomes a Trojan horse
Of grief. Familiar forms will softly creep
And birth the dead, who've long refused to sleep.
They crowd the mirror, leer from dreams, betray
The life we've built atop our phantom heap—
The mourned, the scorned, the loved—the castaway,
Returned to haunt the stage and steal the light away.

XXV.

Enough. My soul, return. Let's face the waste—
The ruin in the ruins, eye to eye.
Among collapsed dominions I embraced
The echo of a grandeur gone awry.
She ruled the sea, and now she rules the sky—
A model posed in marble on despair,
Her mold God's prototype of liberty.
The brave, the beautiful—they breathed her air.
Now ghosts, they ride her bones through tourist-manic glare.

XXVI.

O Italy, thou faded kingdom's bride,
Whose womb bore emperors and Appian roads!
Still art thou art, though whored and gentrified—
Your trash more vibrant than Manhattan codes.
Even your weeds wear diadems like odes.
The rubble of your flesh is pageant-worn;
Your wreckage smells like youth before it explodes—
Where even plague found paradise reborn,
And broke its scythe on columns drenched in dying porn.

XXVII.

The moon is up—but dusk denies its death.
The Alps burn gold, a choral seizure's flare.
All Friuli's peaks draw Heaven's breath—
And Day, not Night, still lingers on the air.
The sky—unclouded—melts to saffron prayer,
An iris bleeding West in smeared delight.
The cosmos, bipolar, blind, laid bare,
Lets Dian float, an isle of gentle fright,
Where gods once lay in shame, then fled from mortal sight.

XXVIII.

A single star, her pimp, escorts her rise,
While sunlight flames upon the Rhaetian peaks.
The Sea—a slut of chrome—still flirts and sighs,
Its Brenta lipstick glistening in streaks.
Here Day and Night enact their tired cliques,
A lovers' spat in violet, bruise, and gold.
Their drama floods the river's sex antiques—
A rose dissolved in perfume, glazed and bold,
Its face submerged in glass, too beautiful to hold.

XXIX.

The heavens press their selfies on the tide—
Each hue, a filter from divinity.
They fade, they blur, they ghost, they twitch, they slide,
And change to shadows, craving symmetry.
The parting Day, in tragic mimicry,
Dies like the dolphin—painted as it chokes.
Its every gasp a new chromatic plea,
Until it's gone, and twilight's cruel jokes
Leave only gray behind, and night, and little hoax.

XXX.

There is a tomb in Arquà, built for lore.
Within it sleeps a lover's praise and pain.
Pilgrims genuflect outside the poet's door,
His bone-thin legend still immune to stain.
He wept in verse, and lived for beauty's name—
A ghost who birthed a language from his loss.
And though his land wore yokes of tribal shame,
He poured out songs like sacramental dross,
And Fame embalmed his voice in aureate gloss.

XXXI.

They keep his dust in Arquà, with respect—
His hut and grave—a dual museum.
The humbleness is all they dare protect,
The sepulchre a shrine, not mausoleum.
It moves the heart because it lacks the tedium
Of monuments erected to self-love.
His memory rests in minor keys of p.m.,
More tender than the tombs that tower above—
His ashes whisper still, with pathos' final shove.

XXXII.

That village where he died—so softly cast—
Feels purpose-built for sorrow's afterglow.
A backdrop for the souls who burned too fast,
Then sought the shade when hope ran dry below.
It gazes down at cities in tableau,
And turns its back on fame's grotesque parade.
The sun need only glint, and time runs slow—
No festival but light; no masquerade.
Here, failed ambitions rot—but ghosts remain well-paid.

XXXIII.

The mountain, leaf, and flower, soft-declared
By rays of God in honeyed camouflage—
Make moral all this languor, unprepared
To climb ambition's final fuselage.
The brook meanders like an old mirage,
Its ripple tuned to time's lethargic hymn.
The calm's not sloth—it's sacred sabotage,
Where Solitude teaches how best to dim
The lights of self, and face the void's unmoving limb.

XXXIV.

Or not. For demons also dwell in peace,
Impairing holy thoughts with gothic grin.
They stalk the mild, the moody, the obese
In soul. They fill the vacuum with their spin.
They make the sun a clot, the air a sin.
Predestined doom they whisper from the start,
And fill the faithful's wounds with devil skin.
Their hell is not beneath—but in the heart,
A deeper tomb where God forgets to take His part.

XXXV.

Ferrara! Oh your streets, all symmetry
Now grassed with silence, wear a prophet's curse.
Your palaces, those shells of royalty,
Held Tyrants who rehearsed their lines in verse.
The House of Este, noble, crude, perverse,
Played God for years behind Baroque façades.
Sometimes they gifted, more they did coerce.
They ruled with smiles that cut like stilett-blades—
A poet's crown their toy, their wrath the artist's spades.

XXXVI.

Torquato—curse and jewel in their crown!
The echo of his strain still haunts your stone.
Look to his cell; look how they locked him down—
His gift, his flame, not theirs to disown.
Alfonso caged what he could not dethrone.
He threw the mind in with the truly mad,
But Glory would not sleep; it made its moan—
The clouds dissolved, and Fame, celestial-clad,
Lit up his name, while all his jailers crawled and clapped.

XXXVII.

His name—a liturgy; yours—silted, drowned.
Torquato's tears still irrigate our speech.
Your dukedom's pageants rot beneath the ground,
While his ignited stars beyond your reach.
Alfonso, damn your lineage! Each leech
That bore your sign is now a historical rash.
If born a peasant, you'd have shined in bleach—
A janitor of souls, with tongue of ash,
Unfit to carry crumbs from Tasso's midnight stash.

XXXVIII.

You lived to eat, be envied, and expire,
A glutton of distraction, drunk on crown.
He suffered light, bled ink, and dreamt of fire,
His furrowed brow a citadel of frown.
Still now it dazzles, burning your throne down.
You fade—he flames, immune to fashion's ire.
Boileau spat shade, the Cruscans wore a frown—
But envy crumbles when its chords retire.
Their verse a whining saw; his—an eternal choir.

XXXIX.

Peace to Torquato's injured, aching ghost.
He was their mark—yet every dart they threw
Missed. He stood tall, the blessed, bastard host
Of wrongs which tried and failed to twist his view.
Millions will rise, but very, very few
Shall wear the crown he wore, and wear it well.
Let ages roll; let poets come anew—
Condense their rays, their scripts, their carousel—
No sun shall rise from them to match his citadel.

XL.

Yet even he—immense—was not alone.
His pedigree was thick with godly ink:
The Bards of Hell and Chivalry had sown
That sacred madness where the righteous sink.
Dante—first cut, the Tuscan Father—linked
To this great line; then Ariosto's call
To love and war in madrigals distinct.
The North had Scott—his minstrel flags and thrall—
Who wrote as if each kiss must be a mortal brawl.

XLI.

But Arno whispers through her white façade—
Florence, that soft dominatrix of the past.
She claims what ruin spared, what gods outlawed;
Her amphitheatre hills still hold her fast.
She pimps out wine and oil, her green recast
As luxury's lush moodboard. Here was born
Commerce's kiss, the Learning once harassed
Now wakes again beneath her Tuscan morn—
Her morning after glow, still drunk on Art's soft porn.

XLII.

Here Beauty floods the air like second skin—
Inhaled as incense, Botox, powdered muse.
The statues glow with secrets held within,
As if the stone could sweat or bleed or bruise.
We stand inside a myth too bright to lose.
Some face, some breast, carved sharp from Pagan ache,
Reveals what even Heaven would refuse—
That Man, when desperate, does more than fake:
He births a god from grief, and begs it not to break.

XLIII.

We stare. We reel. We turn—but not away.
The heart inflates like drugged-up lungs on fire.
Beauty, like ruin, bids us here to stay—
Her leash a chariot, her whip desire.
We stand, new captives to an old Empire,
Where sculpture speaks in silence, not in price.
Forget the marble market's cheap satire—
Our veins affirm the ancient Shepherd's vice:
We too would trade a world for one transcendent slice.

XLIV.

Did you not come to Paris just like this?
To Anchises, drunk on war and starlit hips?
Were you not Glory's heifer, born for bliss,
To whom the vanquished gave their dying lips?
Your lava mouth, your breast where fever drips—
It was not gods but actors you undressed.
And War himself, in armored sponsorship,
Laid down his sword to nap upon your chest,
While Fame massaged your feet and fed your sins with zest.

XLV.

What god could speak of love, when flesh remains
So speechless, so divine in wordless gleam?
Immortal moments flash, then bleed their chains—
A mortal's joy must end the god's regime.
We dream, and build new gods from each lost dream.
The statue holds what time and death let go—
It glows with what we dared not even scream,
A torch from what the soul was forced to know,
And shaped in skinless stone to make its trauma show.

XLVI.

Let scholars ogle thighs and measure grace—
The critic with his ape, all draped in gloss.
They talk of curves with flat, forensic face,
As if pure yearning could be cut or bossed.
They claim to know what you or I have lost.
But let them keep their charts, their sterile schemes—
Their breath defiles the sacred, at what cost?
The form I see is not for thesis-dreams,
But lingers like a flame in pornographic dreams.

XLVII.

In Santa Croce's stone womb lie the kings—
Their dust, if nothing else, redeems the space.
The void is peopled here with ash that sings—
What's left of men who once could shame disgrace.
Here Angelo and Galileo face
A silence carved by genius in its grave.
Here Machiavelli's bones, stripped of his face,
Return to soil like tyrant and like slave,
But leave behind the minds no tombstone dares enslave.

XLVIII.

They were like elements—those four: unbound,
Their lives not lives but templates for a world.
Italy! Though rags have torn your gown,
Your ghosts wear crowns where dukes in shame are hurled.
Time robs all things, yet here your flag's unfurled—
Even your ruins breed divinity.
Canova carves where Michelangelo swirled.
Your fall is not decay—it's pregnancy—
A deathless gesturing to immortality.

XLIX.

But where are Dante, Petrarch, Boccaccio now?
Their bones, we hope, are separate from the herd.
But Florence gave them exile, not a vow.
And though their ink once made her pulse re-stirred,
She left their graves unmarked, their fame interred.
Was there no bust, no godless stone to raise?
Did quarry weep, or sculptor speak one word?
No—only silence, damp with posthumous praise,
Where Genius left no lease, and Fame could not appraise.

L.

Ungrateful Florence—her most sacred ghost
Now sleeps in soil she once denied him near.
Dante, that exiled father—lost and lost—
Whose verses ripped the netherworld from fear.
The factions banned him; Time made him a seer.
Now children mouth his name with sugared awe,
Unknowing Florence dressed her hate as cheer—
The laurel Petrarch earned became outlaw,
And Fame grew wild in lands that never knew her law.

LI.

And Boccaccio, love's heretic and scribe,
Who forged a tongue from music, filth, and fate—
His grave, like his intent, must now ascribe
To vengeance. Bigots broke his tomb too late.
No requiem now—just market rates for hate.
His melody of lust, that siren strain
Which taught the soul to kiss and conjugate,
Is sung in minor key, where ghosts complain—
A song no graveyard hears, but lovers still maintain.

LII.

Santa Croce lacks their mighty dust—how loud
Their absence chants! Like Brutus left from Rome,
Their exile is more sacred than a shroud—
It makes the crypt a chapel, not a home.
Ravenna wins—the exiled saints now roam
Her empire's edge, half-god and half-reviled.
Arquà too cradles verse's holy loam—
While Florence, make-up smeared and Gucci-styled,
Weeps for her dead like any murdering child.

LIII.

What is this pyramid of stones and gems—
This blinged-out crypt for merchant-dukes and fame?
A tomb's a tomb, no matter how it stems—
It cannot cleanse the filth behind the name.
No jasper veil, no agate-lit acclaim
Outshines the turf that gently hugs the dead,
Where poets sleep without a brand or flame,
And grass, not granite, cradles every head.
Their names endure where marble footfalls dare not tread.

LIV.

The lunar strobe descends on ruins dead—
A spotlight dimmed by centuries of spin.
It whispers "here was Rome"—but what is said
Beneath the echo, buried in the din?
She's blind, this night; her daughter, Ignorance, grins.
Maps fail; the stars mock every path we chart.
Knowledge sits wide-legged with wrinkled skin—
Rome is a desert, not a beating heart,
Where every found oasis breaks the soul apart.

LV.

The ghosts, they sob—three hundred triumphs mourned,
And Brutus' blade, that viral act of grace.
Tully's cry and Virgil's myths now scorned;
Livy's page a filter lost in data's race.
Their resurrection lives—but in no place
That stone can hold. The rest is merely dust.
Earth cannot make again that Roman face—
The eyes that once held freedom, not disgust,
Now blink beneath the boot of algorithmic trust.

LVI.

Sylla, who spun fate's wheel and cracked the code,
Who beat Rome's enemies with chilling glee—
His rage deferred, he watched his empire goad
Itself to war; then laid his triumph free.
He shattered senates, smirked at deity,
A tyrant clothed in autocratic light—
Yet in his breath, some brief humanity
That made his sins more vivid in the night—
An antihero's grin in Freedom's stylized fight.

LVII.

Did Sylla guess how small his Rome would shrink?
That one day she would brand what once she bled?
That conquest now means clicks, not sword or ink—
And empire's reach ends where the market's led?
She once threw shadows over all we said.
Now satellites pass through her flaccid reign.
She wore the name Eternal—but it's dead.
The veil was empire; now the veil is stain—
A diva long forgotten by the gods of pain.

LVIII.

And Cromwell, too—the British Sylla's kin—
Who wrecked the crown to found his own control,
Who killed the King, then wore a kingly grin,
His gospel soaked in blood and blackened scroll—
He ruled, then died; his story takes its toll.
We watch the tapes: his triumph, then the loss.
To win the world demands you sell your soul—
To die, perhaps, is sweet—but is the cost
Worth all that blood for freedom's counterfeit embossed?

LIX.

He fell on day three of his destined arc—
His star ascended, then collapsed in sand.
Was Fortune mocking him with that dark mark?
She gives and takes with one Kardashian hand.
All fame is fragile, like a wedding band
Found in a flood. We reach and think it's love—
But once the ring fits, we misunderstand:
The grave, not Fortune, is the prize above—
The crown we dodge below becomes our kiss above.

LX.

And thou—dread Statue!—glaring through the dust,
Where Caesar fell like footage looped in fire.
He tucked his robe; he bled with silent trust,
A viral image framed in brute desire.
Was it for you he died—O stone messiah?
Or for the gods who feasted on that fall?
Was Caesar real, or just the last Empire
Streamed live before the algorithm's crawl—
A puppet crowned, then stabbed to please the ancient mall?

LXI.

O Rome's wet nurse—She-Wolf bronzed and bold—
Your dugs once poured ambition in our veins.
You birthed the breed whose hunger broke the mold—
Whose suckling turned to conquest, then to chains.
The lightning scorched your limbs; your legend stains
The very sky with milk no babe could match.
You watched your children birth their own remains—
Now stand, alone, outside the tourist patch,
Guarding a ghostly gate, too dead for Rome to snatch.

LXII.

But all your pups are martyred into myth—
Men of iron, now memes in minor keys.
We built new cities from their blood and pith,
Then warred for echoes on our bended knees.
They died for fear—we bled for NFTs.
None ruled like them, save one—a self-made god
Who lives, not reigns, by tyrannizing "please."
But he, too, wears the leash his own hand shod—
A king to slaves, but slave to dreams he can't applaud.

LXIII.

A Caesar by design, but bastard bred—
This man, a glitch in ancient archetype.
The Roman had a pulse the algorithm shed;
His heart could bleed, not just absorb the hype.
His flaws were fire; this one's soul is tripe.
The old world's lust now filtered through a screen,
Where even love must wear its chosen stripe.
He posed as Hercules, but dressed obscene—
At Cleopatra's feet, a meme in masculine sheen.

LXIV.

He came. He saw. He conquered—then he sold
The footage rights and hawked the T-shirts twice.
His armies fled like pigeons bought and told
To flap in sync, for drama's market price.
He led them once to glory, now to vice.
And yet, the only flaw that felled his grip
Was not his sins, but vanity's device—
A hunger, not to taste, but just to sip—
And not to own the world, but take a filtered clip.

LXV.

He'd be a god or ghost, but not a name
That Time could blur beneath the parchment's stain.
He craved the arch, the anthem, viral fame—
And let the world bleed red to earn his reign.
The tears of Earth, the universal pain,
All flowed like merch through conquest's showroom gate.
This flood—the same, again, again, again—
No ark arrives, no covenant, no state—
Just blood with every dawn, and death too late.

LXVI.

What fruit is born from this exhausted breath?
We shrink as sense decays; our reason splits.
Life is a blink, and truth must hide from death.
Each value weighed in algorithms, skits.
Opinion rules, while fact in silence sits.
And as the veil grows thicker, right and wrong
Collapse into aesthetics, trends, and bits.
Too bright a thought becomes a viral song—
Then banned before the world recalls it lasted long.

LXVII.

So men decay—each son inherits chains,
Each father weeps for slaves he helped to build.
They bleed for empires inked on primal brains,
Not knowing blood and boredom share one guild.
We kill to feel, then feel to not be killed.
A thousand gladiators spill their guts—
Not for some freedom God or fate distilled—
But just to mimic, like obedient mutts,
The deaths they saw before, rehearsed in endless cuts.

LXVIII.

Creeds are your own—but facts are filtered mass.
What's "true" is what the sponsors deem allowed.
Our yoke is streamed, replayed, then sold as class.
Tyrants now joke in memes, their heads unbowed.
They quote the Lord, then post their abs to cloud.
Their power's not in war, but shameless trend.
The ape now mocks the god who once avowed
To shake the kings from throne and make them bend—
But died before he swiped to see his story's end.

LXIX.

Can only tyrants unmake tyranny?
Does no one breathe like Washington once did—
Born not from birthright but from agony,
And raised not by machines, but forests hid?
The breast of Nature once unlatched its lid
For those who dared to suckle hope and war.
But Europe's sons now rot in beds well-bid—
No Spartans born where death could still restore
The will to live for something more than Prada's store.

LXX.

France drank its blood like absinthe, then it puked—
And cried for gods it murdered in its turn.
Its orgies of the guillotine rebuked
The very star they followed till it burned.
What Freedom saw, Ambition quickly spurned.
The revolution died in scented ink.
The final act: a pageant so well-learned,
It spawned new kings, new chains, new games to link
The soul to commerce, and the state to branded brink.

LXXI.

Still, Freedom limps—her banner torn but high.
She screams against the wind, her lungs half gone.
Her voice, though broken, shakes the blinded sky.
Her blossoms stripped—but sap and roots live on.
A northern seed beneath the bloodless lawn
Still waits to bloom when spring unchains the frost.
Her tree may stagger—but it isn't gone.
And though the rind is dark, and bark is lost—
One bud remains, unbitten by the bitter cost.

LXXII.

There stands a tower—crowned in moss and ghosts,
Its girth untouched by time's desecrating breath.
Two thousand years of ivy haunt its posts—
A fortress wrapped in sorrow, crowned by death.
But not for kings—it guards a girl beneath.
What treasure lies so locked, so unpossessed?
What heart it hid, what face the stone bequeaths—
No one remembers now. They only guessed
A woman slept inside, her silence unimpressed.

LXXIII.

Who was she—queen, courtesan, or pawn?
Her grave's a palace, not a dusty cell.
Did Caesars love her once, or die at dawn
To hold her gaze, or merely wish her well?
What line she bred, no chronicle can tell.
The stone just sighs, a shrine too vast for bones.
She rests in marble where no others dwell—
A ghost more holy than cathedral tones,
A body sealed in fame no death or time dethrones.

LXXIV.

Was she a cipher, saint, or scandal's muse—
This Roman wife, now branded stone and name?
Did duty chain her heart, or did she choose
To wear her virtue like couture, not shame?
Did love go viral in her, or was flame
Denied to her by lineage, will, or dress?
Was Cleopatra's perfume in her frame,
Or Cornelia's chill, her pride, her no, her yes?
We read the face, not soul—she's stylized emptiness.

LXXV.

Perhaps she died when beauty still obeyed
The laws of blush, of flirt, of morning breath.
A single mirror whispered she would fade—
Then dusk arrived, disguised as minor death.
The fever kissed her cheek; she gave it depth.
Her bones were votive, her decline divine.
She wore the veil, not from the grave, but theft—
The gods had claimed her early as a sign:
That heaven fears the bright, and takes them as a line.

LXXVI.

Or else she lived too long, a ghost in pearls,
Who watched her fame decay like ancient grout.
Her hands, once thrones for kiss and ruby swirls,
Now trembled as she touched what Time threw out.
Her hair, gone silver, shimmered still with doubt.
She walked the city—once, her court and cage—
Invisible, save to the stone devout.
What's left? A tomb—a name—a guess—a page:
That she was rich, and loved, or bought, or bought by age.

LXXVII.

But standing here—beside your burial space—
I feel I know you, stranger, though you're sealed.
Your silence speaks like wind on dying face—
A lost refrain, half-mourned and half-revealed.
It's thunder, muffled deep where stars are keeled.
You call me back to versions of myself—
A wrecked desire I thought the past had healed.
I sit beside your stone, like living shelf,
And summon from your void the ghost of dream's last elf.

LXXVIII.

And from the wreckage—scattered love, old scripts,
The ruins of belief—I build a craft.
A bark of hope, where memory slowly drips,
And sails are stitched from images I draft.
It groans against the surge, its rudder daft.
Yet still I steer it toward a phantom shore.
I look for port—but find no gilded haft.
The coast is blank, desire becomes a chore—
The only home I know is what I lost before.

LXXIX.

Then let the storm recite its lullaby—
Its dirge the only music left to feel.
The owl rehearses grief beneath the sky,
Its voice now woven with the night's ordeal.
A chorus mounts upon the Palatine's heel:
The wind, the cry, the echo of a name.
It asks for nothing. It forgets to kneel.
Compared to this, my grief is bright and tame—
Too small to carry weight, too neat to merit blame.

LXXX.

Cypress and ivy—walls like corpses stacked—
The palace kneels in rubble, raped by years.
No fresco speaks, no arch returns the act—
Just shattered colonnades and muscled fears.
The vaults have drowned in subterranean tears.
A temple? Bath? A tomb? What was this place?
No scholar knows—just what the ruin jeers:
The Mountain once was throne, and bore the face
Of Empire's mask—behold! It's now a ruin's case.

LXXXI.

This is the pitch: one story, always told.
It opens sweet—"Freedom"—then curdles fast.
We flash to "Glory" in some chamber bold—
Then fade to wealth, to vice, until the last
Frame flickers—Barbarism—wide and vast.
And History, the franchise of regret,
Rewrites itself with every streaming cast.
Yet here, Rome's moral lingers like a debt:
A palace built from sin, now unpaid, and unmet.

LXXXII.

Cry if you must. Or laugh. Or feel nothing.
This forum breeds emotion like disease.
One minute Rome is noble, pure, and king—
The next, she's ruined, gasping on her knees.
This mountain mocks the centuries with ease.
Its blueprint gone, its architects extinct.
It wore a crown of gold in dreamlike tease—
Now Time, that critic, leaves its fame distinct:
A blistered afterthought, a pixel slowly blinked.

LXXXIII.

You, column—voiceless—are the final word.
Tully's tongue is trivial next to you.
What laurels meant are now absurd, unheard.
Just ivy for my head, where moss grew through.
Whose arch is this? Does Trajan's shadow view
What Time destroyed? No—it's his arch now.
Time mocks the triumphs, flips the stone askew.
His sneer atop apostles makes them bow—
The urn beneath them crushed, like promise, face, and vow.

LXXXIV.

Air-buried urn! You drank the Roman sky—
And looked for kin among the stars, not slaves.
Your breath once summoned gods. Now, dignified,
You float in dusk—half-saint, half-fugue, half-grave.
Your reign outlived the Caesar's viral rave.
He conquered Earth—but you outlived the rule.
No wine, no blood—just virtue's trace you gave.
No scandals dog your name, no hist'ry school—
Still Trajan shines, unspoiled by Time's corrupting tool.

LXXXV.

Where now the altars, plinths, and platforms kissed
By Rome's dead generals, fresh from the wars?
Where stands the cliff where traitors once were hissed—
Then pushed to prove their fall before the stars?
Spoils stacked like bribes, rewards in golden bars—
All echoes now. The field lies hushed in dirt.
Cicero's breath still haunts these marble scars—
His syllables are stone, but sharp—they hurt.
He speaks in vapor now, but still his voice can flirt.

LXXXVI.

This field—this stage of blood and frenzy—sings
Of Freedom gasping in its final scenes.
She came like fire, then drowned beneath the kings,
Then rose again in shadows and machines.
Here passion kissed the Senate's fragile screens,
And mobs like pixels flickered into war.
What followed? Tyrants, laughter, silent screams—
The civic turned obscene, and nothing more.
The forum's script grew rich, then faded into chore.

LXXXVII.

But last, let us invoke that strangest name—
Rienzi!—part mirage, part morning bell.
He rose from ash to renovate Rome's shame,
The people's bard, whose echo rang too well.
He courted fame but ended in a cell.
Too brief a reign—his dream too steep to climb.
Yet still we weave his tomb with verse and spell.
He stood for freedom, in a rented time—
And left behind a myth no tyranny could mime.

LXXXVIII.

Egeria! O blurred hallucination—
A shape born not of blood, but sleepless need.
Were you a woman or an invocation?
A goddess made from tears that couldn't bleed?
Or just a dream, too sacred to recede?
You are desire's avatar in mist—
A grief so soft it doesn't even plead,
But sits where mortal and immortal kissed,
A thought in flesh that only madness could enlist.

LXXXIX.

Your spring survives, and still the moss drinks deep.
The cave remains untouched by manic time.
No sculptor dared its innocence to keep—
It bubbles not in marble but in rhyme.
The waters laugh beneath a godless clime.
No fountainhead for power, crown, or code—
Just liquid breath exhaled in soft sublime,
Where ivy grips the stones that once abode
The echo of a love too luminous to erode.

XC.

So Harold ends—not cleansed, not reconciled—
His path still paved in wreckage, rot, and style.
He bore the mask of misfit and of child,
And wore the cross of exile with a smile.
Each ruin bowed to him—a Roman mile
Of ghosts who recognized their own despair.
Yet in his gaze, there flickered for a while
A glint that mocked regret, denied all prayer:
That life's the only tomb no dreamer gets to spare.

XCI.

He saw the world—a stage without a script,
Where actors bled for laughs or begged for roles.
The stars he chased had burned, their glamour stripped;
Their sparkle just the ash of bygone goals.
He drank from fountains spiked with sainted tolls.
Each city offered him its shrine and vice,
Its Coliseum dreams and Tarquin scrolls—
But nothing gave him peace, nor fair device
To staunch the truth: all beauty comes with sacrifice.

XCII.

Yet still he roamed—not out of need but form.
To stand still was to die, to breathe was flee.
The soul, like coin, must tarnish to be warm—
And Harold spent his on eternity.
The ruins now were mirrors, not decree.
He saw his face in every empire's fall,
And understood the cost of being free:
To lose yourself in marble's voiceless call,
And find, in dust and dream, the only rise is crawl.

XCIII.

So here we part—in Rome, beneath the moon,
Where laurels rot and lilies dare to grow.
The tale is done; not ended, just too soon—
A reel that loops, where nothing new will show.
The world reboots in grief, in afterglow.
The poet fades, his ink outlived by death.
But whisper, if you must, before you go:
That once he walked through time without a breath—
A ghost who mourned the gods, then gave them back his flesh.

XCIV.

O Love—thou ghost who never knew the skin,
A rumor whispered through our orphaned bones.
No heart has touched thee—only dreamed within,
And made of thee a myth, a mobile phone's
Last text unsent. No cherub sings, no thrones
Are thine; just phantoms conjured by despair.
We shaped thee from our ache, our silent moans,
And gave thee flesh to haunt the perfumed air—
A mask the soul wears out, then strips beneath its care.

XCV.

The mind creates what never can exist,
And calls it beauty—fever-born and blind.
Where is the form the chisel could not twist,
The face the mirror never dared to find?
Where are the truths the dreamer left behind—
The virtues sketched in blood when boys were kings?
We draw them still, on screens, in hope designed,
But every brushstroke tears, not mends, our wings—
We paint our Hell as Heaven, with the same old things.

XCVI.

To love is madness, but to cease is worse;
Each charm that once adorned now mocks the eye.
We peel away the glamour like a curse,
And find no god, no truth beneath the lie.
Yet still we chase, though knowing love will die.
The mind, a moth, insists the flame is pure,
Though every wing is ash. We scream and sigh—
A wound that wants to spread, but not to cure—
Enchanted by a prize that ruins the rich and poor.

XCVII.

We rot from youth—our fever never slaked.
We chase the thirst until the lips decay.
Some ghost returns, a hunger half-awake,
A phantom flashing through our final day.
We die as we began: in sad display.
Love, Fame, Ambition—all are apps we scroll,
Each lit, then gone—each flare a fake delay.
The flame burns out, and Death reclaims the whole—
Just ash where passion played, just smoke where once was soul.

XCVIII.

Few find what they desire—they touch, then lose.
Blind chance pretends to grant, then takes away.
What seemed like love becomes a shattered ruse—
The hand once warm now stings in disarray.
Wrong follows wrong, each born from yesterday.
And Circumstance, that bastard god of trend,
Creates new plagues, then limps to make us pay.
Hope turns to sand no algorithm can bend—
A broken crutch we lean on, never to ascend.

XCIX.

Life is a glitch—a coded fraud, a mess.
This virus called Original Despair
Infects the stars, the root, the small redress
We beg from Earth. The sky pretends to care,
But rains down plagues we never saw were there.
Disease, deceit, and bondage drip like dew.
The woes we name are nothing to compare
To those that fester deep and have no hue—
The ache we cannot name, yet feel the whole life through.

C.

Yet let us dare to think—that final flame
Still flickers when all else has curled in dust.
They say "believe," but that's the dealer's game—
I choose to reason, even if it's just
A flame in wind, a cry in broken trust.
Though shackled from our birth in cell and sin,
The eye will open if the gaze is just—
Time is the surgeon; truth the light within—
Let blind men look to stars, and call it not a sin.

CI.

Rome builds her ego in concentric rings,
Each arch a filter, each arena fed
By blood once spilled for sport and crown of kings—
The Colosseum stands, not raised but bled.
The moon now lights it like a priestess wed
To Death. Its vaults still echo with despair.
This ruin feasts on thought, not flesh now shed,
But minds collapse where once fell limbs laid bare—
A temple to regret, to ghosts, to godless prayer.

CII.

The night wears robes of blue that speak in flame—
Not heat, but hues that conjure ghosts of sky.
The monument beneath this whispering name
Still murmurs myths to every watcher's eye.
Time's hand has grazed it, breaking yet not dry.
There's power here—unnamed, yet not untrue.
The past still pulses though the present lies—
And pomp dissolves when ruins claim their due,
While palaces today await what time will do.

CIII.

O Time, embalmer of the desecrated—
You polish bones and make decay sublime.
Your hands are velvet where the blade once grated—
You kiss the corpse, and make it worth the crime.
You straighten what we bent; you bloom in grime.
You wait, you smirk, you never truly fade.
And though the world forgets the loss in time,
You archive every sorrow ever made—
And wear the tears of men like diamonds never paid.

CIV.

Here where the marble crumbles into myth,
I give my years—though brief, still steeped in doom.
These ruins mirror mine; they fade forthwith,
Yet shine in loss, like perfumes at a tomb.
If once I laughed, let no god hear me fume.
But if I bore the fire without complaint,
Then let me keep my soul—its iron gloom.
No hatred shall erase this dark restraint—
If Rome forgets to mourn, I shall not play the saint.

CV.

And thou, Nemesis—rage with better grace—
O ancient force who punished without haste.
No guilt escapes your scales, no crime your face.
You summoned furies once to track and taste
Orestes' blood—you hunt but do not waste.
Now hear me cry in ruins long your seat—
This ground is just; the sky, your old estate.
Let no remorse, no modern mercy cheat—
Awake and walk again with vengeance on your feet.

CVI.

It may be I deserve the blade I feel—
If not from me, then from the fathers' sin.
But justice wears no mask, and will not kneel
To bloodlines. Strike—but strike with hands akin
To truth, not treason. Let the war begin.
If I must bleed, let every drop be heard.
The vengeance owed is not to me, but kin—
To all who suffered long without a word—
The grave may take my voice, but still it shall be stirred.

CVII.

If I should speak, it will not be to plead.
I suffer—yes—but let no eye presume
To see me wilt. The pain is not my creed,
But merely shadow dancing round the room.
I etch these words as curses, not as gloom.
Though turned to ash, this verse shall not erase.
A day shall come when these lines bloom—
And every wound shall rise to take its place,
As justice rains in tongues, and mercy wears no face.

CVIII.

And what's that curse? Forgiveness. Yes, that bane.
To pity what we cannot bear to touch.
O Earth—my witness—and you stars that reign,
Have I not hurt enough? Have I not clutched
At ghostly straws and found no grace in such?
My name defamed, my love betrayed, my will
Bent to the point of fracture—scarred too much.
And yet—I walk. I live. I wander still—
Not damned enough to die, nor sainted by the kill.

CIX.

From slander's bellow to betrayal's hiss,
I've known the full-range score of human rot.
The smile that hides the fang, the Judas kiss,
The silent nod that kills while speaking not.
The shrug that damns, the pause that means a lot.
They feign respect, then stab without the deed.
They praise your art, then sell your soul for plot.
The lie wears silk; the truth is made to bleed—
Yet still I speak—I write—I curse—and still I read.

CX.

But I have lived, and living carved a brand
That time and torture cannot strip or sell.
Let death arrive—I'll greet it, not demand—
For what I bear transcends this mortal shell.
I am the echo fame forgets to quell.
I am the chord still thrumming in the cave.
What breaks me only rings like poet's knell—
And even they, who watched me die, shall crave
The pulse I left behind—the art they could not save.

CXI.

Now come, unnamed—but not unloved—Dark Power.
I see you in the colonnade, the dust.
You walk at midnight, and your touch devours
The past with velvet gloves and breathless trust.
You haunt the stone with sweetness edged in rust.
We walk together now, unseen, allied—
In you, I see my own reflected lust
For what has gone, and never will abide—
We merge, one ruined god, one ghost too tired to hide.

CXII.

Here once the masses cheered as blood was spilled—
The murmur of the mob—a savage choir.
Their pity feigned, their hunger never filled,
As gladiators danced through flesh and fire.
And why? Because the state required desire.
The sport of kings was death in public view.
We still applaud—just different brands of pyre—
New apps, new screens, but still the same review:
To kill, to watch, to cheer—what else is there to do?

CXIII.

I see him—leaning—noble in his fall.
No martyr, just a man denied his breath.
The cut is deep, but deeper is the call
To meet his fate with elegance, not death.
Each drop, a psalm. Each gasp, a shibboleth.
Around him swirls the crowd's last, brutal cheer.
He dies as all men do—beyond all myth—
The world indifferent, though the cut is clear.
The crowd forgets. He fades. His silence meets the spear.

CXIV.

He heard their roar—the human algorithm's cheer—
But all he saw were ghosts by Danube's tide.
Not prize nor pain could draw his vision near;
His mind had fled to where his children hide—
Two sons, still pure, a wife unsold by pride.
What is a crown to one who fed his kin?
This blood was his, not Rome's, and still he died.
Their hashtags hailed his death with crooked grin—
"Just content," screamed the crowd. Let vengeance now begin.

CXV.

This was the app where blood went viral fast—
Where crowds were metrics, gladiators' likes.
Each death a post, each cry a trending blast;
The pit a feed refreshed by swords and spikes.
But now it echoes, hollow as the strikes
Of wind on ruin's ribs. These seats, half-torn,
Once throbbed with rage and joy in metric hikes—
Now emptiness replies where cheers were born,
And every step I take is past a ghost reborn.

CXVI.

A ruin, yes—but what a ruin stands!
Its bones still breed erections in the mind.
This carcass fathered palaces and brands
Of war and gospel, all from rot designed.
No, Time has not erased—it's just refined.
Each crack reveals the rot that once was grace.
The form survives; the soul is not aligned.
Expose it all—let sunlight strip the place:
What time devours, the world still markets as a face.

CXVII.

But let the moon ascend this broken arch,
That hooded voyeur of the sacred trash—
Its light more kind than day's invasive march,
Its hush more holy than the daytime clash.
It stains the walls in silver wounds and ash;
The laurels rot on Caesar's empty head.
Yet in that gleam, the graves renew their flash—
The heroes stir, disturbed within the dead,
And tell us that we walk where empires bled.

CXVIII.

"While stands the Coliseum, Rome shall stand."
A prophecy now pimped in tourist ink.
"Rome falls—the world falls." So speaks Saxon brand—
A slogan carved in selfie-precious brink.
But nothing stands; it only learns to shrink.
The ruin thrives because we film it fall.
Redemption? No. Just ruins made to think
That rot is noble when it's built this tall—
A grave that tweets: "The world is thieves, or not at all."

CXIX.

Erect, severe—a shrine of hybrid gods,
Where Jupiter met Christ in shared despair.
Its ribs outlasted emperors and frauds;
Its shell survived Time's tantrum, priest and heir.
The Dome still domes, despite the thinning air.
Man ages through it like a crawl through flame—
His ashes caught in fresco, frame, and prayer.
No tyrant cracked its skin, no war its name—
It holds our past intact, but never quite the same.

CXX.

A relic—yes—but not of time alone:
Of genius raped, of art that dared too much.
Its aperture bleeds light like holy bone;
A wound that glows with beauty's final touch.
No altar spared, no bust without a crutch.
Yet here the dreamers find their soul's display—
A Pantheon of ghosts and those who clutch
At genius like a relic gone astray,
Each face a shrine to art that would not stay.

CXXI.

There is a crypt where shadow feeds on light—
At first, just blackness. Then, like blood through gauze,
Two shapes congeal: a man, long lost to night,
A girl beside—death's paradox, death's clause.
Their silence speaks what law can never pause.
The girl's unmantled breast, the old man's face—
Both shine where pity fails, and shame withdraws.
Why is she there? Not lust, nor cruel disgrace—
But life itself reversed in one obscene embrace.

CXXII.

From her, the milk—Edenic, full and live.
No doctrine births such beauty as this flow.
To give what once was taken, now to give
Again—her body speaks what prayers don't know.
Man cannot feel this ache—he can't bestow
The holy tremor in a nursing sigh.
Her child is bud, and she the tree below—
But even trees must wonder, by and by,
What fruit will bloom from love—when Cain was Eve's first try.

CXXIII.

Here, youth feeds age—not metaphor, but meat.
The daughter nurses sire—not sex, not myth.
No man shall die while milk can still compete
With death—her veins run hymns, and he drinks pith
Of mother-love from daughter's breast. What if
This tide outlives all gods, all tombs, all creed?
This Nile of flesh, not bound by scripture's glyph,
Restores the blood, the bond, the primal need—
A daughter's gift that even Heaven's tide can't breed.

CXXIV.

Your Milky Way is fable, faint and far.
This moment births a deeper constellation—
Not stars, but veins—no sky, just breast and scar.
What galaxy can match this new salvation?
No priest, no martyr's tale, no revelation
Can echo what her body dares to prove.
No fount more sacred than this aberration:
A child becomes the vessel of her love—
A soul returned, as blood repents what time can't move.

CXXV.

Now look—Hadrian's Mole, that mimic tower,
That fat ambition rising from the Nile.
It wears its Roman bluster like a flower—
A monument to vanity in style.
The artist groaned; the emperor just smiled.
His ashes lie within, still shrunk and proud—
But God laughs hard at mortals who compile
Their tombs in marble, thinking death allowed
A second chance to rise before the final shroud.

CXXVI.

And there—the Dome. That swollen, holy beast,
Built high above the martyr's final breath.
I've seen the ruins of the East, released
To wolves and jackals lounging under death.
Sophia's glitter dulled by mosque and myth.
Ephesus, strewn in weeds and sacred rust.
Each temple crowned with absence, scorn, and myth.
But this one breathes—it does not weep or trust—
It sells its awe in scale, and trades its soul in dust.

CXXVII.

Of altars old, this temple stands alone—
Unrivalled in its size, its gloss, its game.
God left Jerusalem—this was his throne.
Since Zion cracked, no architect could claim
A worthier vault to house the holy name.
Strength, Beauty, Glory—every Art aligned
To make this vault a brand, this dome a flame.
What temple rivals this? None yet designed.
This Ark endures—the flood left all but it behind.

CXXVIII.

Enter—it will not crush you with its scale.
It stretches you instead, makes vast your mind.
You feel your body swell, your breath inhale
A new immensity, until you find
The Infinite is merely redefined.
Your soul expands—each step, a liturgy—
Until, if God appears, you are not blind.
You meet Him, not in fear, but clarity:
A mirror in the Dome, that shows divinity.

CXXIX.

Advance, and feel it grow. Each arch, each line,
Deceives by grace—like Alps, they seem to end,
Then rise again. Each altar's hue, divine—
Each vault reveals a heaven to defend.
And though the Dome ascends where eagles send
Their cries, it grounds itself in human need.
You climb, and climb, until the clouds suspend
The dome above your doubt, your daily creed—
You rise, a supplicant whose breath becomes a bead.

CXXX.

Yet grandeur here is no mere boast or mask—
It burns with awe beyond the reach of scorn.
The Dome does not demand; it dares to ask
If man was made to suffer or be born.
No creed, no flag, no epigraph adorn
The truth that speaks from every arching beam:
That power bows to silence, not the horn—
And every saint who knelt within this dream
Was just a man who dared to love his God obscene.

CXXXI.

And I—I wandered here not out of faith,
But habit, ache, and tourist disbelief.
My sins were not absolved, nor was I wraithed
In light. I brought no prayers, no page of grief.
Yet something stirred beneath the gilded leaf—
Not piety, but longing undefined.
It hummed beneath the apse, the cleric's brief,
A hush not preached, but whispered through the mind—
A voiceless voice, not God, but what He left behind.

CXXXII.

So let the priests proclaim their endless wars,
Their rituals of incense, robe, and blame.
Let choirboys bleed in frescoed corridors—
The Dome endures, untouched by human shame.
Its reach exceeds the sins that bruise its name.
No scandal spoils the blueprint of the skies.
It is not God, but awe that fuels its flame,
A thunder built from shape, not from replies—
A space too vast for truth, too holy for the wise.

CXXXIII.

And now, my pilgrimage dissolves in dusk.
The stones still warm with saints I'll never meet.
Rome fades behind, half-haunted and half-brusk,
Its ruins coiled beneath my aching feet.
The sky withdraws; the moon prepares retreat.
I leave no relic, verse, or tear behind—
Just footprints, lost where marble meets the street.
The Dome still looms, but I've gone blind to mind—
A shadow leaves the world, and none were made to find.

CXXXIV.

Behold the archer—sun-split, flame-forged, bare—
Not man, but myth in dermal hologram.
He lifts the bow with Adderall despair,
His glare a crypto-god's encrypted jam.
He aims not down—but through you, where the spam
Of history clots in cells of light and loss.
What majesty in hate, what nerve, what glam—
His shaft is truth, his silence severs dross—
He is the Deity made flesh through violent gloss.

CXXXV.

Yet in that form—so poised, so veined with lust—
A fever dream from some Narcissus nymph—
We see not wrath, but love: profane, robust,
The ache of myths who wear no modern lymph.
He gleams like avatars in heaven's pimp.
Each pose an algorithm of desire—
Each breath a chord to which the angels limp.
He was a God before the flesh caught fire,
And stardust posed as skin to let us once aspire.

CXXXVI.

And if Prometheus, bro-coder of fire,
Stole from the cloud a sacred viral stream,
Then here it found its host—an antique wire
Of marble wit, half-vigil and half-dream.
This stone does not decay, it seems to scream—
A meme before the age of endless scroll.
This flame was forged not by a priestly scheme,
But by the hand that shaped a broken whole—
A statue lit by pain, with hope as its control.

CXXXVII.

But where, O where, the Pilgrim—my mirage?
The one who wandered as my soul's disguise?
He looms no more; his file corrupt, his charge
Expunged by time. No avatar replies.
He was a ghost in flesh, a fraud in cries.
His scroll ends here, his storyline expires—
Unless he was a lie behind my eyes,
A phantasm fed by trauma and desires—
A silhouette dissolved in history's damp choirs.

CXXXVIII.

Now all is shadow: voice, intent, and name.
The archive closes; silence spreads like blood.
We birthed our myths, then watched them die the same—
Each prince, a hashtag drowned beneath the flood.
Glory? A tincture blurred in viral mud.
We saw her die—mother and meme and lie—
Not murdered, but out-clicked in global thud.
Her halo dimmed, reduced to lullaby—
The kind that makes us weep, but none recall just why.

CXXXIX.

We probe the void to see what's left to lose—
Some brittle fame, a name no longer said.
The soul? A concept hidden in a ruse—
The shell long cracked, the heart presumed as dead.
And still we dream—of tweets that could have led
To love, to truth, to meaning's phantom gate.
But what survives? The sweat we barely shed—
Our burden: not to rise, but simulate
The self we once believed was more than fear and fate.

CXL.

Listen—the abyss speaks back, a latent hum,
A tremor built of wars and breastless queens.
A cry not screamed, but sampled, bass and drum,
As if the world were scored in grief's machines.
She stands there still, the matriarch of scenes—
No crown, no milk, no God to mend the pain.
Her child stillborn, her empire wrecked in memes.
She lifts the babe to breast, but finds disdain—
A womb that bore the world, now voided for no gain.

CXLI.

Where is the Scion? Monarch of the viral dream?
The last blue-blooded hope in bloodless land?
Can't death have taken some less-trending meme?
But no—he fell. And with him, all things planned.
The Isle now mourns what pixels couldn't brand.
No mother now, no joy remains to stream—
Just funeral hearts, black-robed and shamed and scanned.
The future, once a feed of royal gleam,
Now buffers slow beneath the coffin's cryptic theme.

CXLII.

The peasants birth with ease, yet queens expire.
No cure for irony, no balm for class.
We weep not for the crown, but for desire—
That image born in screens, now gone like gas.
We prayed for her, and now she's GIF and mass.
You, lonely Consort, father without heir,
Your dynasty unbirthed, the dream won't pass.
What year begins with widower's blank stare—
A Lord bereft of flesh, now bound to vapor's care?

CXLIII.

Her wedding veil was stitched with funeral thread,
The bride's bouquet composed of ash and rue.
Her child, the ghost of every tear we shed,
The heir of grief the algorithm outgrew.
We saw her smile; now we refresh the view.
We thought her child would reign beyond our death—
But meteor's shine is brief, and leaves no clue.
We watched her fall and swallowed all our breath—
The Isle now dreams in black beneath its scented wreath.

CXLIV.

We mourn for us—not her. She sleeps in peace,
While we must scroll through endless autopsies.
Her fate was mercy—brief and clean release;
Ours is to linger in these viral seas.
Kings fall from tweets. The mob demands its fees.
No throne survives the algorithm's weight.
And she? Too young, too fair for fates like these.
She left before the meme became the hate—
A saint without a scandal, too pure for her state.

CXLV.

No prophecy can hold the grief she wrought.
From throne to tenement, the pulse went dead.
Her loss, a circuit broken into thought—
A nation blinked, a pixel wept, and said:
"She was too soft for all the blood we bled."
The king himself, unwed in soul and skin,
Now walks in shadow through his golden dread.
The people grieve, yet know not where to begin—
For how can love be mourned when grief is built within?

CXLVI.

And now—Nemi. Wound of the wooded hills.
So deep, the storm itself forgets to howl.
A lake that dreams in glass—its surface stills
All rage, all wind, all gods who used to prowl.
It coils like vengeance in the viper's cowl.
No ripple speaks; no light defiles its face.
It is the eye of nature's final scowl—
A mirror held to time, to shame, to grace—
Too calm for joy, too vast to leave a trace.

CXLVII.

Albano, twin in silence, burns afar.
And Tiber weaves its elegy below.
Rome shivers, ghostless, underneath its star—
Each ruin sings the songs we used to know.
"Arms and the Man," now drowned in TikTok flow.
Tully's repose, the Sabine field's delight,
Are apps we swipe and never dare to show.
What once was farm or forum now is blight—
A filtered past too real to face, too faint for fight.

CXLVIII.

But I digress—the shrine is reached, the tale
Now cracks apart beneath the weight it bore.
The Pilgrim dies, his shadow worn, his grail
An empty script he's read too many times before.
We turn to sea, that primal metaphor.
From this high mount, the waves like pixels gleam—
A final reel before the credits pour.
We watched it start beneath Calypso's dream,
And end, as all things do, in silence, tide, and scream.

CXLIX.

Years passed—not many, but enough to rot.
The damage subtle, but the core was stripped.
What had we gained? What gods, what wars, what plot?
We came full circle, broken, bound, and clipped.
And yet, a sliver of the sun still dipped
Its warmth in us. The sea, the rock, the sky—
They let us dream, though hope itself had slipped.
And though the world was lost, we did not die—
We dared to call it love, though love had passed us by.

CL.

O to retreat into the mythic sand,
With one fair shade to soothe the final itch—
No likes, no names, no bloody hashtag brand,
Just solitude, and her—my soul's last glitch.
Ye Elements, reboot me from this glitch!
Let one true thing remain amidst the spam.
A voice, a breath, a tremble at the switch—
Some memory before I ceased to am,
A lover in the void, not part of program's scam.

CLI.

There is a hush within the endless noise,
A rapture in the chaos of the shore.
No chat, no ping, no broken plastic toys—
Just ocean's scream, more ancient than the war.
I do not hate the world—I want no more.
These walks, this drift, these microbursts of sky—
They take me back to what I was before:
Not man, not code, not product made to lie,
But just a breath, a tide—a cry that did not die.

CLII.

Roll on, O Sea—thy darkness knows no bot.
Ten thousand fleets dissolve, but thou remain.
The world decays in code—thy death is not.
Man ruins all, but never drowns thy vein.
Thy wrecks are honest, born of storm, not brain.
His name will fade, as all his apps expire—
But thou art deathless, part of God's disdain.
Thy grave is void. No coffin, priest, or pyre
Can catch the soul that sinks in thee and won't retire.

CLIII.

He walks not on your waves. You shake him off.
His cities sink. His myths return to clay.
You sneer at missiles, memes, or monarch's scoff—
They perish, while you lap in ancient play.
You toss his corpse like driftwood, born astray.
His prayers, his screams, his tools—they fall like dross.
You do not kill him—you just turn away.
And send him not to heaven, but to loss—
That blank, unholy peace the cosmos names as "cross."

CLIV.

His arms, his warships—thunder-born and vast—
All crumble like a snowflake in thy spume.
His conquests rot in silence, nothing cast
But data logs to mark a future tomb.
He calls thee "Lord," and yet you spell his doom.
He thinks he rules; he does not know the rules.
Each empire ends in you. Each hero's plume
Becomes your foam. Each genius joins the fools—
A tide that drowns us all, but still we build our schools.

CLV.

Thy shores have seen it all—Assyria's screams,
Carthage ablaze, Rome choking on its fame.
The sea endures; its silence breaks our dreams.
Its waves erase what history dares to name.
Greece, crushed beneath the global branding game.
And yet you roll—unchanged, untouched, unseen.
No monument escapes your fluid claim.
Each statue drowns, each scroll becomes routine—
You cleanse what men corrupt, and make the past obscene.

CLVI.

Thou art no god—but something deeper, rawer.
The mirror not of Heaven, but of It.
You storm and freeze and boil—not by a law,
But by a rage that doesn't give a shit.
Thy monsters rise from algorithms split.
Each zone obeys—each realm dissolves in foam.
You do not preach, you do not ask, submit.
You are the throne, the tomb, the endless dome—
The womb of horror, yes—but also Heaven's home.

CLVII.

And I have loved you, Sea—since I was child.
You were my solace, fear, and restless friend.
With you I broke, with you I reconciled.
I rode your waves, your tantrums without end.
And still you take me in—still you unbend.
My hand upon your mane, as once before—
We meet again, no need to now pretend.
Though all I was has drained upon your shore,
You keep my final truth, the one thing I adore.

CLVIII.

The poem dies. The ghost dissolves. The light
That flared in me is flickering to ash.
I end as I began—in silent fight,
In verses scrawled like wreckage in a crash.
The torch goes out; the script becomes a splash.
And yet, if in your breath remains a phrase—
Then let it float. Let it not turn to trash.
I was not great. I only tried to blaze—
A wound that burned in ink, a loss that sought its praise.

CLIX.

Farewell. The voice departs, but not the sound.
You followed him—the Pilgrim—through his strain.
If even one of you was faintly bound
To what he saw, then none of it was vain.
The song is done. It will not rise again.
Let him go down into the sea of scroll.
Let me dissolve, my ache a fading stain—
The Moral his, the silence now my role:
A whisper made of blood, a verse to end the whole.

www.ingramcontent.com/pod-product-compliance
Lightning Source LLC
Chambersburg PA
CBHW032054090426
42744CB00005B/212